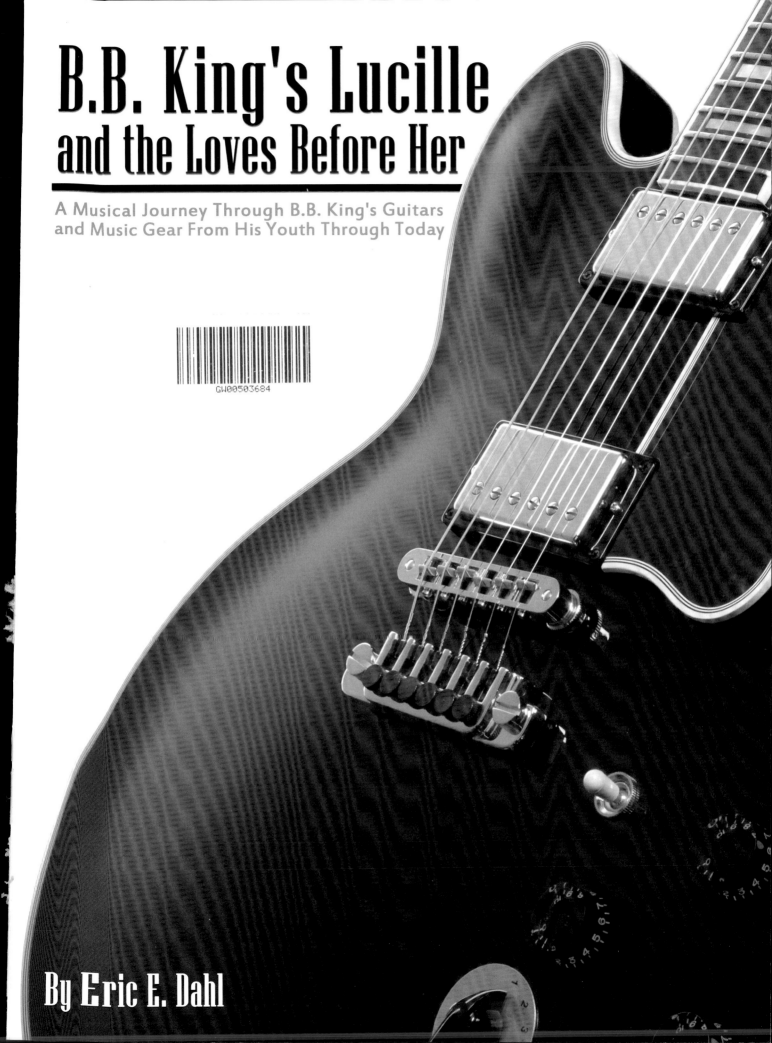

B.B. King's Lucille
and the Loves Before Her

A Musical Journey Through B.B. King's Guitars
and Music Gear From His Youth Through Today

GW00503684

By Eric E. Dahl

COPYRIGHT, GENERAL INFORMATION, AND ABOUT THE COVER

BLUE BOOK PUBLICATIONS, INC.
8009 34th Ave. S., Ste #250
Minneapolis, MN 55425
Phone: 800-877-4867
Phone: 952-854-5229 (International)
Fax: 952-853-1486
Website: www.bluebookofguitarvalues.com
Email: support@bluebookinc.com

Published and printed in the United States of America

MSRP: $17.95

ISBN: 1-936120-41-0

EAN: 978-1-936120-41-3

ABOUT THE COVER:

The guitar pictured on the cover is obviously a Gibson Lucille guitar in the ebony color most favored by B.B. King. It is at one point simple but also elegant with smooth flowing lines like a fine automobile. It is the culmination of years of effort from numerous Gibson employees and Mr. King to build his dream signature model guitar incorporating elements from each favored instrument that he played and owned up until 1980, when she was officially launched into the Gibson line and introduced to the world. Mr. King told me in person how much he loved his Lucille and she continues to be a faithful companion to him to this day!

The title of this book was a joint venture. *Lucille and the Loves Before Her* had been my working title for the book for some time, but thanks to Zach Fjestad's suggestion we changed it to start with Mr. King's name so it would be easier for people just like you to find it.

B.B. KING'S LUCILLE AND THE LOVES BEFORE HER CREDITS:

PRODUCTION MANAGER & ART DIRECTOR: CLINT H. SCHMIDT

EDITOR: ZACHARY R. FJESTAD

COVER LAYOUT & DESIGN: CLINT H. SCHMIDT

COPYEDITING & PROOFREADING: KELSEY FJESTAD, CASSANDRA FAULKNER, & ZACHARY R. FJESTAD

PRINTER: BANG PRINTING, BRAINERD, MN

TABLE OF CONTENTS

DEDICATION BY AUTHOR

This book is dedicated to the late Jerry Dahl, my father, mentor, and inspiration. He had the heart of a musician and a passion for the blues that he instilled in me at a young age. I am forever grateful.

Jerry Dahl and the author jamming in 1982 in Fruitland, Missouri, after high school graduation.

ACKNOWLEDGEMENTS

Thank you is a token of appreciation to everyone that provided their guidance, encouragement, and advice while writing this book, and I apologize that I can't mention everyone. B.B. King, thank you for giving me the privilege to meet you in person and to write this book! Also thank you to Ms. LaVerne Toney (VP B.B. King Road Shows) for always being kind, answering my endless questions, and being a liaison between me and Mr. King! Thanks to my mother and father for making music a part of my daily life growing up. My wife, Les, has been incredibly supportive and understanding during late night research, weekend interviews, and general writer frustrations – I Love You!

I believe my family and friends had more faith in my completing this book than I did in myself and I appreciate you all! Thanks to everyone that gave their time and patience in allowing me to interview them and enrich the stories and details in this book. Also thanks to my personal advisors who help guide me through life's rocky path. My spiritual advisor, Pastor Don Lorfing of Good Samaritan Lutheran Church in Las Vegas, your prayers, words of wisdom, and listening mean a lot! Joe Lowes, my Guitar Buying/Life Advisor, has been like an older (much older) brother to me since I was five years old. Joe's advice has always been "Buy It," and I think that was the right call as several of those guitars are mentioned in these pages. The staff and management at my publishing company, Blue Book Publications out of Minneapolis, have given me great guidance and support! Especially Zach Fjestad (Author/Editor) who encouraged me the entire time I was writing and researching this book to complete a sentence a week and never stop or give up on the dream.

And thanks to you, the reader, for purchasing this book! My goal in writing it was to provide a timeline of Mr. King's music gear and guitars and showcase some of the incredible people behind the scenes that create and maintain these instruments. I never really thought of writing a book before, but after doing so much research on B.B. King and his guitars it seemed like the only logical choice. I am truly blessed with the family and friends I have and the new ones that I have acquired while composing this book. Thank you!

FOREWORD BY B.B. KING

I have owned many guitars in my lifetime, but I am most proud of my Gibson B.B. King Lucille signature model that they make for me to this day. This book talks about some of my past guitars that finally led up to my final Lucille. It also goes into my favorite amps and some of the other stuff I use to make music. Although I believe most of my sound really comes from my fingers petting on Lucille. You'll also find the story in here about Eric returning my stolen Birthday Lucille, which means a lot to me. I am blessed to still play the blues to people who want to hear me all over the world and to have played with some of the best musicians on this earth.

B.B. King

ABOUT THE AUTHOR

Eric E. Dahl was born in Peoria, Illinois, as his father and grandfather had been, but he was raised in Southeast Missouri. His fascination with guitars and the blues started at age five since both parents had exceptional taste in music and his father worked his way through college as a bass player. Eric played music with many local bands through his formative years, and after graduating high school, he moved to Nashville, Tennessee, to pursue a degree in music at Belmont College. After one semester, he decided radio and TV might be a more stable source of income, so he returned to the Midwest and achieved a BA in mass communications and a music minor in jazz/classical guitar from Southeast Missouri State University. His career in television has led him from working at a local FOX affiliate in Cape Girardeau, Missouri, to pursuing promotions in Las Vegas, Nevada, and finally back to Nashville, Tennessee, all with the same company and spanning almost 30 years!

Eric has been a performing musician and guitar collector for over 40 years. He is a Contributing Editor for Blue Book Publications and has had articles appear in numerous publications. He is also an Instrument Value Appraiser for music stores and pawnshops in Nashville and Las Vegas. Eric has one daughter, Taylor, and currently resides in Nashville, Tennessee, with his wife Leslie, a cat called King Tut, and a Bassett Hound named Mrs. Potts. 👑

INTRODUCTION BY RICK VITO

It was November 1968, and I was home visiting my parents when I got the news from my "blues friends" that none other than the great B.B. King would be performing that very day on DJ Jerry Blavat's TV show in Philadelphia. Four or five of us piled into my car, sped down Township Line to the station, got in, and took our seats. There weren't many there that day to see B.B. and the main guest, Mel Tormé, but we, being big fans, were not about to let that bother us. After sitting through a long interview and a couple of songs by Mel it was finally time for B.B.!

We watched as B.B.'s band quickly set up and before we knew it, there HE was…the man…larger than life. With his beloved Lucille (this time a shiny red Gibson ES-345), B.B. took center stage and waited for his introduction. Jerry made mention of the fact that B.B. was gaining fast popularity with youth all over the country and when we at last heard his name, we in our seats made sure that we were going to give our idol his props, applauding and screaming wildly. B.B. went right into "How Blue Can You Get?" and Lucille's sweet tones blasted out through his Fender Twin Reverb amp, filling the station with that signature sound, complete with all his trademark vibrato and trills. After the line, "I gave you seven children and now you wanna give 'em back," we got so loud that both Jerry Blavat and Mel Tormé turned in their seats, astonished that this man was getting this kind of response from a bunch of young guys. I don't know how well they knew who B.B. King was prior to this performance, but by God, after it was over they sure did. We raised so much ruckus with our enthusiastic clapping and hollering that it must have sounded like the studio was completely packed to the rafters. Jerry came over and asked if we'd like to come back tomorrow, and we told him we would if he'd have B.B. King again. Then all at once to our left standing next to us was B.B. himself, actually thanking us for coming and for "being responsible for him being seen in such a good light." Wow…this man was the King of the Blues in our eyes, but at that moment we saw what a humble, lovely gentleman he truly was, and we were honored beyond belief. He invited us to walk out to the van and I took the opportunity to ask if I could carry Lucille, and B.B. said I could. I carried LUCILLE! A young lady, perhaps his daughter, was waiting in the

Rick Vito is a world-renowned blues guitarist and singer who is best known for his stints in Fleetwood Mac and Bonnie Raitt's touring band. Being a blues musician, Vito cites his influences as Les Paul, Keith Richards, George Harrison, and B.B. King. His slide guitar work can be heard on Bob Seger's song "Like A Rock," and he has played with several other musicians as well. Vito has a signature Reverend guitar and currently tours with his own band making frequent appearances at vintage guitar shows across the country. Image courtesy Rick Vito

band vehicle and I told her I admired the fact that she got to hear this great man every night. She said, "Oh, if you had to listen to that old blues stuff every night you wouldn't think it's so great!" I've thought about her saying that a thousand times since then, but never once have I ever thought that the sound of B.B. King and Lucille wasn't the greatest signature voice the blues has ever produced. To this day, I marvel at the purity of guitar tones B.B. has always been able to coax out of all the different Lucilles. But then again, I know for sure that no matter what guitar he is playing, the real instrument of B.B King is found deep in the heart and soul of the man. ♛

Chapter 1
ONE STRING AT A TIME

Riley B. King was born September 16, 1925, on a farming plantation in Itta Bena, Mississippi, to Nora Ella and Alfred King, but that is not where our story begins. This is not a tale of a man and his never-ending quest to spread the gospel of the blues across the four corners of the earth. This is about tools – musical tools of the trade that are used to build melodies, chords, emotions, and songs instead of a nice walnut cabinet.

Stringed instruments, whether as musical bows or chordophones, have been created and played with since 3000 BC dating back to the times of the Sumerians and Egyptians. Through the years, they evolved from single string bows and harps to violas, vihuelas, and eventually the Spanish guitar, which led to the guitar as we have come to know it today.

In the early 1900s, there was a transition from Classical and Flamenco guitars to the American Folk Steel string guitars, which provided more volume for the music of the day. But if you were an African American tenant farmer living on a plantation in the post-Civil War South, your opportunities to find and play instruments were far fewer and limited. Many plantation owners didn't allow their workers to own or play any kind of instrument for fear they would communicate with other workers on other plantations and form organized revolts against them! But the passion, and need, to create and make music was more powerful than the methods used to suppress it. To make music, people were forced to either use their voices to sing or improvise by building their own crude instruments, such as drums and fretless banjars that could be made from items around the farm. Thus was born the need to create the Diddley Bow, a single stringed version of a guitar. Typically, the Diddley Bow was made by driving two nails or screws into a porch beam, broom handle, or a two by four approximately a foot and a half apart. Then a piece of wire, usually fence wire since it was readily available from the farm supplies, was tightened to various pitches by twisting the wire and putting a shim (sometimes a piece of wood or a small bottle) up underneath it. The one string zither, as some people called them, would then be played using a glass bottle, screw driver, ham bone, or any other hard object that could be slid up and down to change the pitch of the string. It was played like a Dobro or resonator guitar, but with only one string compared to six. As many early blues artists from the 20th century started their musical careers this way, this instrument usually led to the guitar next as the single string was very limited and no chords could be created while playing it. Such was the case with Riley B. King as he lived on the plantation with his mother, Nora Ella King, in the early 1930s. B.B. has stated, in his authorized biography, that his first instrument was a Diddley Bow when he was a pre-teen. King told LaVerne Toney, VP of B.B. King Road Show Productions, "Many of the young guys played [the Diddley Bow] because they had no money and they were making fun [having a good time] with them!" ♛

The Diddley Bow is the simplest version of a guitar. It features one string strung between two nails with a glass bottle used to change the pitch as it is slid back and forth. The Diddley Bow was King's first instrument before he was a teenager. Image courtesy David Williams, a.k.a. One String Willie.

Chapter 2
B.B.'S FIRST GUITAR

In approximately 1937, B.B. King was a hard working teenager of 12 years old and had begun saving his money from working in the fields and his willingness to pick extra cotton for money.

His first guitar was "a little Red Stella" that he paid the price of $15 to acquire (a full month's work at that time), which he later felt was more than the student model guitar was worth.

The Stella Guitar Company has gone through several incarnations in its long history. Stella (the word means "Star" in Latin) was originally owned by the Oscar Schmidt Company, which was founded in 1899. Since the Stella name was acquired by Harmony Guitar Company of Chicago, Illinois, in 1939, it stands to reason that B.B.'s first guitar was built at the end of the Oscar Schmidt production years.

For most of us, the Stella brand brings to mind cheap 1960s entry-level guitars that seldom stayed in tune and frequently needed a neck or bridge reset, but when the Oscar Schmidt Co. was creating them they were of much higher quality. This also explains why many blues artists from the 1920s and '30s performed and were pictured playing Stella models and how the brand has become synonymous with the early emergence of blues music. By the late 1930s, the Stella and Sovereign brand names were both acquired by the Harmony Guitar Company, which built and distributed them through the 1960s.

It is interesting that the Stella guitar was also the choice of one of B.B.'s early guitar idols, Blind Lemon Jefferson, who was known for playing a 12-string model of the guitar. Oscar Schmidt led the market for 12-string production as they launched them prior to WWI and continued through the 1930s. Musicians like Lead Belly, Blind Willie McTell, and of course Blind Lemon Jefferson embraced these 12-strings and kept them popular even as six-string guitars started exceeding them in popularity.

Mr. King's model was more than likely one of the basic Stella models where the entire guitar was constructed from birch, although the fret boards were usually made from pear wood, birch, maple, or poplar,

and then dyed a darker color to give the illusion of rosewood and ebony. His model would have been a standard or concert size, which was the most popular model for this time, and featured a width of 13 in. to 13.5 in. at the bottom and had a 25 in. scale neck. These guitars featured 12-fret necks with simple dot position markers and a flat fret board. Stella guitars like these were known for their loud volume to help accompany the blues vocals, and they were a cheaper alternative to the much more expensive metal body National guitars of the time period.

B.B. King recounts that his Stella guitar was later stolen from the cabin he lived in on the Mississippi plantation while he was out working the fields. After this hard lesson of having his first prized guitar stolen from his own home, it was several years before he bought a replacement guitar.

The Oscar Schmidt-built Stella guitars, such as B.B.'s, have become very collectable and are commanding impressive prices in recent years. Neil Harpe, out of Annapolis, Maryland, is a great resource on these guitars and wrote a book about them; if you own or are considering acquiring one of these instruments, it's a must read. ♔

Stella guitar in Red circa 1930s - similar to B.B. King's first guitar! Courtesy Neil Harpe

Chapter 3
KING'S SECOND GUITAR

Although details are sketchy on B.B.'s second guitar, it was more than likely another early model Stella that he purchased for $20 so he could accompany the Famous St. John Gospel Singers gospel band (when asked he didn't recall what kind of guitar it was since it was so long ago). Even though his guitar frequently kept him and his band out of many churches, as the guitar was felt to be too harsh an instrument for gospel music, B.B. persisted in playing it. Very little is known about this guitar except for one photo with the entire band from the 1940s and a mention in King's autobiography that he wrote with David Ritz: *Blues All Around Me*. In an old surviving photo, he appears to be holding a vintage resonator-style guitar, but we don't know if this was used for a prop for the photo or if it belonged to him. Upon closer inspection, the guitar pictured could be a Regal or Dobro since at that time many of the instrument manufacturers shared parts! Either way, this was just an in-between instrument as he would soon move on to electrifying his sound to reach more listeners! ♔

This is the only known picture of B.B. King with the Famous St. John Gospel Singers gospel band taken in the 1940s. Pictured to the right in the back row, King has what appears to be either a Regal or Dobro resonator. Image courtesy Charles Sawyer

Chapter 4
THE GIBSON L-30 GUITAR THAT BECAME LUCILLE

By the age of 15, B.B. bought his next guitar for $30, a lot of money in 1940, and it was definitely a step toward the quality of guitars he would play in the future. This guitar was a Gibson L-30, which he eventually added a DeArmond pickup to so that he could amplify it for house parties and his radio gig, but I'm getting ahead of myself on that. The Gibson L-30 was first introduced in 1935, and was discontinued in 1943, as provided from *Gruhn's Guide to Vintage Guitars*. It featured the simple silk screened Gibson logo of the time at the top of the headstock, single binding on the top and back, along with a flat back and arched top, simple dot inlays, matching f-holes, and a simulated tortoiseshell pickguard with no binding. The body size was 14 ¾ inches, which was the same as its big brother, the L-50, and it also had an adjustable bridge, which helped with tuning and intonation. It was offered in Black or Sunburst finish at the time, but B.B.'s was a Sunburst. This was the same guitar that he played to entertain on the radio station WDIA in Memphis. It was here where King got his nickname, "Beale Street Blues Boy," which was later shortened to B.B. and even down to B with close friends and family.

The L-30 served him well and eventually took on a new name and persona of its own after a house party in Twist, Arkansas. As the story goes, as told by Mr. King himself, he was playing a house party one night in the winter of 1949. To heat the room, the owner had placed a large bucket of kerosene in the middle of the room and lit it on fire to knock the chill of the season. A fight broke out between two men over a woman and the bucket of kerosene was knocked across the floor, causing the entire building to catch on fire. Everyone, including B.B. King, ran out from the house to get away from the fire. Then B.B. remembered he left his prized possession and his <u>only</u> guitar inside the burning structure, so he ran in and retrieved it, barely saving his own life much less his guitar. The next day, he found out that the fight was over a woman named "Lucille."

Although he never met the woman in person, he named all of his consecutive guitars after her to remind him to never do something so foolish again,

like running into a flaming building to save a guitar. Unfortunately this "Lucille," as with several others over the years, was not destined to stay with King for very long. While traveling through Buffalo to visit a friend, he left his guitar in the trunk of his Oldsmobile. Unbeknownst to King at the time that night, the same key would fit most General Motors cars that year. Not only was "Lucille" stolen, but also his amplifier and the battery to his car! B.B. has been quoted as saying that he offered a $5,000 reward and all the way up to $10,000 for the guitar's return, but no one ever did collect the reward. He would give $100,000 for its return today, but feels that since his name wasn't on it the thief never even knew whose guitar they stole. So the original "Lucille" (a modified and well played and loved Gibson L-30) is added to the long list of Stolen Celebrity guitars that were never returned, but this was only the beginning of "Lucille's" long legacy. ♛

A Gibson L-30, similar to B.B. King's first Lucille. Courtesy John Beeson - The Music Shoppe

Chapter 5
THE FENDER YEARS

For obvious reasons, none of us have heard much about B.B. playing a Fender, mainly because he only utilized the brand for a short portion of his musical career and ever since then he has been faithful to the Gibson Guitar Company. Over the years, many people have mistaken B.B. King's Fender guitar for a Telecaster, and it has even been mislabeled in several published articles, books, and online, but it was actually a Fender Esquire.

Simply put, the Esquire guitar was the beginning of the Fender family tree that led to the evolution of the Broadcaster, No Caster (due to a lawsuit by the Gretsch Company), and eventually the Telecaster (named in reference to the new entertainment provider of the era–television). Although the neck, body, and controls are the same as the Telecaster, the main difference is that the Esquire only has one physical single coil pickup in the bridge. A number of Leo Fender's prototypes and testing guitars have turned up over the years, but the Esquire was the first guitar that he introduced to the public in 1950. It had a limited run since the originals were produced without truss rods and the model was eventually replaced by the Telecaster due to necks warping. Some other famous Esquire players have included Luther Perkins (Johnny Cash guitarist) and Bruce Springsteen. The first Esquire prototype was finished by Fender in late 1949. Features included a flat slab body with a single cutaway allowing easier access up the fretboard than many jazz-style guitars offered at the time. True manufacturing of the Esquire guitar began in April of 1950, and it appeared in Fender's spring catalog. B.B. made a huge leap from a jazz-style guitar such as the Gibson L-30 to what was considered the radical styling of a solid body Fender Esquire guitar with a bolt-on neck. It is probable that King still pulled some of his favorite Gibsons into service during this period, but at least recording for the RPM Label from 1950 through 1957, his primary recording tool was the Fender Esquire that he was pictured with during this time period. 👑

B.B. King shown holding a Fender Esquire guitar during his RPM recording years.

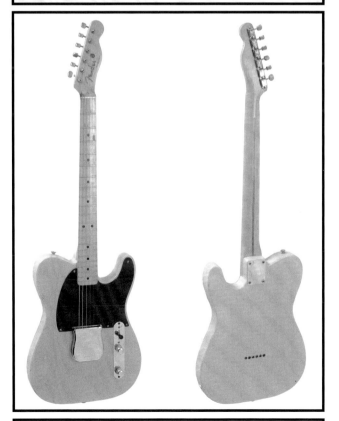

A Fender Esquire guitar. Courtesy Dave Rogers - Dave's Guitar Shop

Chapter 6
KING RETURNS TO GIBSON

I t seems like more than coincidence that B.B.'s return to the Gibson line of instruments happened the same year that the Gibson ES-335 model was introduced into production in the Kalamazoo factory. After his brief brush with Fender, King returned to his familiar old friend Gibson around 1957-58. It has been documented, through interviews, photos, and recordings, that B.B. has played a wide variety of Gibson guitars during his extensive career. Some of these include the ES-175, ES-5, Byrdland, ES-330, ES-335, ES-345, and the ES-355.

Gibson has been very fond of using letters as abbreviations for words in the titles of their guitars. In this case the "E" stands for electric and the "S" stands for Spanish, which was the standardized phrase for their electric guitar offerings that were originally arch top guitars with a pickup added. As we inch closer to the creation of King's signature model, we will also see "T" used for thin line, "S" for stereo output, "D" for double pickups, and "V" for the Vari-Tone circuit. The higher the number designation reflects the increased number of cosmetic upgrades such as neck inlays and multi layer binding; this is observed in the ES-125 series (considered a student model) while the ES-355 was considered the top of the thin line series. Eventually, the 355 would also be out done by the artist signature models such as Lucille. The upcoming chapters will touch on the guitar models and styles that B.B. spent the most time with and that led up to the creation of the Lucille. In the span of playing for over 70 years, it would be virtually impossible to touch upon every single guitar King has laid his hands upon, but every effort has been made to bring details and information to light on his most favored instruments! 👑

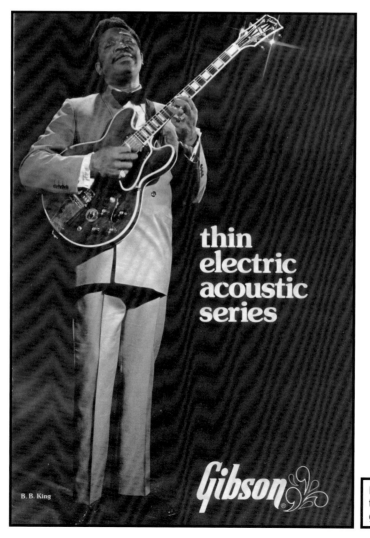

thin electric acoustic series

B.B. King

Gibson

B.B. King appears on the cover of a Gibson guitar catalog, 1975.

Chapter 7
GIBSON ES-5 GUITAR

It would be logical to assume that B.B. King gravitated to this particular model to emulate one of his guitar idols, T-Bone Walker, who played it as his primary instrument for most of his illustrious career. Besides being an incredible musician and showman, Walker picked behind his back, did splits, and picked with his teeth before Jimi Hendrix. T-Bone is also considered a pioneer for using an electric guitar and amplifying it. Another habit that T-Bone exhibited, and B.B. embraced, was the use of single string lyrical lines as a way to play guitar solos!

The Gibson ES-5 model was introduced in 1949, and featured a large 17 in. wide body, triple P-90 pickups, three volume controls, and one master volume control. It is considered a Full Depth model in *Gruhn's Guide to Vintage Guitars*. King started playing this model in the early 1950s and can be seen in a classic stage picture from that time period where he is decked out in cool shorts, shoes, and a jacket while strumming his ES-5 through a Fender amp to the left of him! The Gibson ES-5 Electric Archtop was produced from 1949 to 1962, and it has been reissued by Gibson over the years. In 1957, humbucker pickups replaced the original P-90 configuration, although the earlier instruments are considered more collectible by purists and the P-90 model was the one B.B. owned and played.

As with many Gibson guitars, it is tough to get an exact count on the number of ES-5s produced, but production numbers are considered low. It was a very impressive looking and sounding guitar back when it was launched and still is today. Although it was designed to be an ultimate jazz guitar, it crossed genres with a number of musicians. Huck Daniels, who was also a friend of T-Bone Walker, got to play his ES-5 before it was stolen while on tour in France. Huck said, "It was one of the lightest and best sounding guitars I ever played and those hound dog P-90s sure were sweet." Many top notch bluesmen still swear by the tone and subtleties provided by these vintage P-90 pickups! ♔

A Gibson ES-5 guitar. Courtesy Dave Rogers - Dave's Guitar Shop

Chapter 8
GIBSON BYRDLAND GUITAR

A Gibson Byrdland guitar.
Courtesy Dave Rogers - Dave's
Guitar Shop

B.B. continued to sample from the Gibson well of guitars and he turned his attention to the Byrdland. Some experts feel the Byrdland, which was named after legendary guitarists Billy Byrd and Hank Garland for their input on creating it, was Gibson's first move towards their highly sought after thin line series, or "ES" standing for Electric Spanish. Players of the time were tired of playing Gibson's thicker body offerings and wanted something that was more comfortable. The Byrdland addressed these concerns and included a single round cutaway, multi-bound hollow body, solid spruce top, raised bound tortoiseshell pickguard, bound f-holes, maple back/sides/neck, multi-bound ebony fingerboard with pearl block inlay, tune-o-matic bridge, trapeze tailpiece, multi-bound blackface peghead with pearl flowerpot/logo inlay, three-per-side tuners, gold hardware, two single coil Alnico (disc. late 1957) or humbucker (introduced 1958) pickups, two volume/two tone controls, three-position switch, available in Natural or Sunburst (more common) finish, mfg. 1955-1985.

It should also be mentioned that this is currently the main guitar of choice for King's touring rhythm guitarist, Charlie Dennis. Having been allowed to play Mr. Dennis' guitar myself, I was truly amazed at how comfortable the guitar felt in your hands and on your lap, and how effortlessly you could play chords and solos! Sitting on a guitar stand, and in the hands of Charlie, it looks much more intimidating. It is truly a playable work of art by the Gibson Custom Shop. It is no surprise why a guitar of this caliber was part of King's guitar journey on the road to his ideal instrument. I had a chance to buy one of these, cheap and used, from Kenny Martin at Shivelbines Music in Cape Girardeau back in the 1990s, and I still regret passing up that opportunity to this day! ♛ᵣ

Chapter 9
GIBSON ES-335 GUITAR

There are a number of pictures of B.B. King playing the Gibson ES-335 model in the 1970s. This was the beginning of King's introduction to the Gibson thin line models, which he has stayed with for the rest of his musical career. The first ES-335 guitars came out in the spring of 1958, and although they weren't an immediate hit (much like the Flying V, Explorer, and Firebird models when introduced), they definitely caught on with the rock generation in the late '60s. Besides featuring a thinner body than King's L-30 or ES-5, the ES-335 model had a double cutaway, double humbucker pickups, two volume controls, two tone controls, and one pickup selector. It also had a solid wood center block, which made it less prone to feedback at higher volumes – something that has always been a challenge for King. Even after switching to the ES-335, it has been documented that B.B. would fill the f-shaped sound holes with newspaper, socks, or anything else he could find to fill the interior guitar space and control the feedback he would get on stage at the high volumes he played. Most of the ES-335 attributes carried over to his eventual signature model including the guitar body shape and dual humbucker pickups.

Milton Hopkins and Huck Daniels, two of B.B.'s studio musicians in the 1970s, both used Gibson ES-335 guitars on his albums. Huck's was a Red 1968 model that he played through 1979. He now plays an Epiphone Sheraton with 59er Gibson pickups in it to get close to his old sound. Much like a Gibson Les Paul or a Fender Stratocaster, the Gibson ES-335 is an iconic instrument that has been played by such guitar heroes as Eric Clapton, Stevie Ray Vaughn, Elvin Bishop, and of course Mr. 335 Larry Carlton! ♔

This 2009 Gibson ES-335 produced in Gibson's Memphis factory is very similar to the ES-335 B.B. King played during the 1970s minus the Bigsby vibrato tailpiece. B.B. King was known for filling up the f-holes on this guitar to try to eliminate feedback when he played! Image courtesy Gibson Guitar Brands

Chapter 10
GIBSON ES-345 GUITAR

A Gibson ES-345 guitar. Courtesy Dave Rogers - Dave's Guitar Shop

Much like human or animal evolution (if you subscribe to Darwin), B.B.'s taste in guitars over the years continued to evolve toward what would become his signature model "Lucille," and the ES-345 is one of the dominant links in this progression. The ES-345 model, a step up from the 335, was launched in 1959 by Gibson and stayed in production until 1982. Features included the standard double rounded cutaway semi-hollow bound body, arched maple top, unbound f-holes, raised layered black or tortoiseshell pickguard, maple back/sides, mahogany neck, 22-fret bound rosewood fingerboard with pearl parallelogram inlay, tune-o-matic bridge (bridge system designed by Ted McCarty for the Gibson Les Paul guitar in the 1950s), trapeze tailpiece, (Bigsby tailpiece available as custom order), blackface peghead with pearl crown/logo inlay, three-per-side tuners with plastic buttons, gold hardware, two covered humbucker pickups, two volume/two tone controls, three-position/Vari-Tone switch (in 1959, the six position Vari-Tone switch that filters out center frequencies to allow the guitar to sound differently was offered on this guitar), and stereo output (made it possible for you to run your sound through two different amplifiers at the same time).

The upgrade features that remained from B.B's guitar's ancestor to his eventual signature model were the Vari-Tone switch and the stereo output as he frequently ran two amps on stage.

In 2002, the Gibson Custom Shop in Memphis created the ES-345 Reissue (ES45), which was designed to reproduce B.B.'s original ES-345. Features included all of the standard ones listed above plus gold hardware and it was offered in Transparent Brown, Transparent Red, Faded Cherry, Triburst, or Vintage Sunburst finish. 👑

Chapter 11
GIBSON ES-355 TD-SV GUITAR

The Gibson ES-355 TD-SV was the final link that led B.B. and Gibson to the creation of his own signature model "Lucille." In fact, King was featured on the cover of Gibson's Thin Electric Acoustic catalog for 1975. Besides being affiliated with B.B. King, other guitar players of note such as Freddie King, Frank Zappa, Chuck Berry, and Alex Lifeson also wielded the Gibson ES-355 TD-SV guitar, although it became synonymous with King thanks to his live performances and Gibson's extensive advertising in the 1960s and '70s! What is also interesting is that a number of the features that were so popular on the 355 were used as a basis for the eventual B.B. King Signature model by Gibson. These included: ebony fingerboard, pearl block inlays, gold plated hardware, tune-o-matic bridge, twin humbucking pickups with separate tone and volume controls for each pickup, three-position toggle switch (to choose each pickup by itself or together in the middle position), and Vari-Tone and stereo or mono output capability. The Vari-Tone, besides offering different filtered frequency ranges, also offered one position that had no effect on the guitar sound.

Huck Daniels, a local Las Vegas blues musician and friend of B.B.'s, played with King in the mid-1970s. He stated, "B.B. had two of the ES-355 TD-SV guitars when we were recording in the studio. Both of them were all black and he would record with his main one and always kept the backup in its case, on the chance something went wrong." Huck isn't a big fan of the Lucille model and feels that King got his best tone back when he played live and recorded with the ES-355, which had more of an open tone from its hollow wings

and f-holes. Daniels said, "Gotta have that hollow sound, he [B.B.] lost tone when he went with Lucille." In King's mind, I think the solid top without f-holes that he requested specifically on the final version of "Lucille" was one more step towards his dream guitar that he had been in pursuit of since he was a young man. Many musicians and music critics would argue to the contrary that King's tone and sustain actually increased after the production of his own Gibson guitar model. ♛

B.B. King featured in a 1970s Gibson guitar ad.

Chapter 12
B.B. KING'S SIGNATURE GUITAR

Orville Gibson first brought Gibson instruments to America in the 1890s, in Kalamazoo, Michigan; this is also the site where Gibson gave birth to B.B. King's first signature series guitar in 1980, almost 100 years later. As B.B. found features that appealed to him from each of the Gibson guitars that he played over the years, he never found one instrument that encompassed all of those details in one instrument. One of the most bothersome problems he was plagued with in virtually every Gibson semi-hollow body he played was frequent bouts of feedback caused by the open f-holes on the guitars' tops. Per the *Blue Book of Electric Guitars*, "The first B.B. King models were introduced in 1980 with two variations: the B.B. King Standard and the B.B. King Custom. Rather than true signature models, these guitars were regular production models with King's personal touches, and have never been part of Gibson's Artist collection. The B.B. King models are based on a Gibson ES-345 with Vari-Tone stereo electronics. Each model was renamed in 1981, respectively as the Lucille Standard and Lucille Custom. The Standard was produced through 1985, in 1986 the Lucille Custom was changed to the B.B. King Lucille, and up until 2002, and there was only this variation of the B.B. King." But these are just production facts and guitar geek details for people like me – the real story lies with an old friend of King's from the 1960s.

Chapter 13
LUCILLE'S GODFATHER

He has been called "Lucille's Godfather," a name given to him by none other than B.B. King himself – but friends, family, and fellow musicians know him as Dennis Chandler, the Professor, or just D.C. as I have known him. Of all the people I have interviewed for this book, he is probably one of the most interesting, charismatic, and a wealth of musical knowledge on Gibson and many other things. I learned many fascinating details about Gibson, Norlin, and the Kalamazoo years from him. Based out of Solon, Ohio, you can't grasp how influential Chandler was to the music industry, unless of course you happened to come across his personal website like I did!

D.C. first met B.B. in 1965 when he went to see him play at Leo's Casino in Cleveland, Ohio, and Chandler became the student and King the teacher and mentor. Early on in this close friendship, D.C. vowed to B.B. that "he would be the one to get Gibson to make a signature model for him." This went on for ten years and King would allow D.C. to sit in and jam with the band on piano as part of his schooling. D.C. kept to his promise by writing letters to Gibson requesting that they create a B.B. King Lucille starting in 1975. Apparently this letter caught the attention of Bruce Bolen, Gibson Marketing Executive at that time, and he responded back to D.C. since B.B. suggested that he should. D.C. seized this opportunity, (after having 12 years of banking jobs) called Bruce, asked for a job at Gibson Guitars, and as they say, the rest is history. D.C. was hired in to replace Joe Browne, one of the "Old CMI (Chicago Musical Instruments, another music company owned by Gibson in the '70s) guys." He quickly climbed the ranks at Gibson, becoming a District Sales Manager over Cleveland, Pittsburg, Atlanta, Toledo, and Columbus. So in 1979, D.C. won the Gibson Sales Contest for the year, which included an incentive trip to the Contadora Islands in the Bahamas with then President of Gibson, Bob McCran. While they were out sailing on the ocean with McCran, Marty Walk, Jim Whithall (Gibson VP), Bob, and Chandler, D.C. said, "I got a favor; it's time to have a Lucille in the line." To which McCran simply said, "Great idea, go do it!"

Photo by Liz Chandler

Dennis Chandler and B.B. King on King's bus after a show. Courtesy Dennis and Liz Chandler

After returning from the trip, D.C. held the first meeting with Gibson Executives and B.B.'s manager, Sid Seidenberg. The next meeting about the guitar occurred after one of King's gigs at the fabled Front Round Theater (in Cleveland, Ohio) back stage. Upon being told that Gibson would create the first B.B. King signature Lucille model, King raised his hands over his head, looked to the sky, and said, "Dreams come true!"

From the beginning, D.C. said King was a fan of the Gibson ES Artist model, but with no tailpiece (usually attached at the bottom of the guitar and the strings run up through it) and instead liked the stopbar tailpiece (two bolts are secured through the top of the guitar body and the strings run through a piece of metal in between the bolts). I asked D.C. why Lucille was launched with a TP-6 fine tuning tailpiece (all six strings rest in individual channels and can be fine-tuned from the base of the guitar in smaller increments than the machine heads at the headstock of the guitar). He said the only reason was that it had just been introduced at that time so they added it on! King would always take the tremolo off of his 345 and 355s. He told D.C. he liked the TP-6 bridge because he could tune it with his right hand while playing. Dennis stated that B.B. wasn't very technical, which he will admit to you in person, when it came to his likes and dislikes on a guitar – but he knows what plays and sounds right to him.

As they were working out the details, D.C. brought vintage necks from Kalamazoo and King's favorites were a 1968 and 1969 355 style neck. He also "preferred red walnut for the neck on the prototype 355." D.C. told me the early 335 necks were made from mahogany, but B.B. "liked the feel of the maple better." King made it known that he wanted to keep the Vari-Tone circuit from the 345/355 models on his signature model. "We started with a stripped down 355 and B.B. liked the ebony fretboard for its smoothness best and big block inlays," D.C. said. Other details B.B. requested at the time were: "He likes a traditional bone nut, not a brass one, strings break off the bridge at a 20% angle, fret height a little higher than medium (to provide better left hand vibrato)." D.C. and the team had drawn up illustrations of most of Lucille's crucial areas, and King preferred that the mother of pearl inlay in the headstock be in script. When they were originally launched, the Standard model had chrome hardware and the Custom model had gold (like King played and preferred). I asked D.C. why they offered a model with chrome hardware at all and he said it was to offer a price break, but it diluted the market. D.C. said, "People want what their hero plays – exactly!"

As you can find in the *Blue Book of Electric Guitars*, from 1980-82 the Gibson Lucille was just referred to as the Lucille with no other identifier. Originally it just had block letters on the truss rod cover to signify what it was. The solid top Lucille with no f-holes was an obvious choice for B.B. as D.C. had seen him use "newspapers, cardboard, or whatever else was handy," to fill the sound holes of his other Gibsons since King "didn't like squealing." Since its inception, other than varying paint jobs, inlays, and headstock veneers, the original design of the Gibson B.B. King Lucille has remained the same since it was launched in 1980–a testament to Dennis Chandler, his team of luthiers at Gibson, and B.B. King knowing what he required from a player's perspective! Even though it took 15 years (1965-1980) to make it a reality, it still amazes me that D.C. (with all odds stacked against him and

not even working at Gibson yet) was able to pull off a promise that he made to King of creating a Signature model guitar for him one day. Some things are obviously meant to be, and the creation of Lucille as a Gibson Signature Series production model was one of them.   Here are the specifications for the B.B. KING STANDARD/LUCILLE STANDARD from 1980-85 from the *Blue Book of Electric Guitars*: symmetrical double rounded cutaway ES-335-style semi-hollow body, arched maple top, maple back and sides, no f-holes, multi-ply top and back binding, maple neck, 22-fret bound rosewood fingerboard with pearl dot inlays, black headstock overlay with pearl Gibson logo and Lucille inlays, three-per-side tuners, tune-o-matic bridge, TP-6 tunable stop tailpiece, raised layered black pickguard, two covered humbucker pickups, stereo electronics, four knobs (two v, two t), three-way pickup switch, two 1/4 in. outputs, chrome hardware, available in Cherry or Ebony finish. ♔

Dennis Chandler's B.B. King autographed Gibson ES-355 TD-SV. Courtesy Dennis and Liz Chandler

Chapter 14
TONY COLEMAN – B.B. KING'S DRUMMER/PERCUSSIONIST

Tony Coleman has played with King, more on than off, ever since he was originally hired January 5, 1979, while still playing with the Otis Clay Band. Coleman's famous father, Canton (King) Coleman, was also a famous musician and is known for "Mashed Potatoes – Part 1". Tony had known and seen B.B. for a number of years before this since they moved in the same circles with such blues luminaries as Buddy Guy, Junior Wells, Albert King, Charlie Musselwhite, and Bobby Blue Bland.

One night after they had played a gig at the Burning Spear, the after party was held at the High Chaparral club. It was B.B.'s birthday celebration, but the band that was playing wouldn't do another set unless they got paid more money. So Otis went around asking all of the artists, including B.B., to sit in and play. This was the first time Coleman got to see Lucille "real up close" as he puts it. Bebop, the manager and knocked out horn player, was told by King to go get Lucille and let Leonard Gill make her "whine." Tony recounted, "Leonard got up to go play Lucille but sure was nervous to handle her."

Tony Coleman performing as B.B. King's percussionist. Courtesy Ann Marie Pezzulo

Coleman has a lot of good memories of traveling the world with B.B.: "The road and people he plays for are like family. It's like he invites you to his home!" As other King band members have told, B.B. is very serious about his job. Tony said B.B. told him once, "When I'm on stage, I have no friends on stage when it comes to messing up!" Besides interviewing him, I also got the chance to see Tony back up King live in 2011 at the Ryman Auditorium in Nashville, Tennessee. Coleman held B.B.'s rhythm section together like a rhythmic artist, and never got a mean look from B.B. the entire show!

Unfortunately, as frequently happens with bluesmen and their sidekicks, Tony Coleman and Mr. King parted ways in March of 2013. Herman Jackson, Randy Jackson's brother from *American Idol* fame, is now B.B.'s percussionist on the road. At this writing, Tony has a new found energy for producing and writing again! Besides helping to guide new artists like Ana Popović and Tre Williams, he is also playing in a few side projects as well! As Coleman put it to me, "I'm now playing all the different flavors I like covering more funk than blues!" With Tony's incredible ear and eye for talent, I'm certain we will hear more from him and his musical disciples in the future.

Tony Coleman performing behind B.B. King at a concert. Courtesy Ann Marie Pezzulo

Chapter 15
GIBSON B.B. KING ONE OF A KIND 70TH BIRTHDAY LUCILLE

Just when I think things can't get any stranger as I pursue the elusive "Lucille" and the different guitars that B.B. King has played, another Lucille oddity finds me. This is like one of those fishing stories where I say, "You should have seen the one that got away!" As I became more immersed in the Lucille models, I was in one of my local vintage guitar haunts called Cowtown Guitars in Las Vegas. The owner, Mark Chatfield, has been a touring guitarist with Bob Seger since 1983, and now resides in Oklahoma. They had several standard model Lucilles come through the shop in the past few years, sometimes three at once, so I tried to stay up to date by checking their website and by making periodic visits across town to their shop.

After walking in the front door, I was greeted by the oddest looking Lucille I have ever seen in my life hanging on the wall, and it featured a crudely written "Not for Sale" sign on a piece of rough, torn cardboard. I got the guys manning the store to pull it down and let me see it in person and snap some pictures with my cell phone. Up close, it looked more like a promotional guitar for B.B.'s Blues Clubs than it did a special or custom model dedicated to him. (Mr. King co-owns Blues Clubs in Memphis, Nashville, Orlando, West Palm Beach, New York, and Las Vegas, and per Jason Toney, B.B. is contracted to play in each one a minimum of twice per year).

The features included the names of some of his hit songs inlayed into the mother of pearl fretboard, a picture of B.B. inlayed into the body, a unique headstock, his birth date carved into the gold plated truss rod cover, and to top it off it had f-holes (which no manufactured Lucille model except for the Little Lucille has had). Another unique feature, of the many on this model, is that Gibson added an input jack to the back of the body to accommodate King's method of sitting while he plays now. The store manager was told by a Gibson representative that 50 of these were created in 1995 to commemorate B.B. King's 70th birthday, but I have not been able to verify this through any other sources.

Several months after seeing the Cowtown example of this guitar, I contacted the store to see if I could come by and have professional pictures shot for my book, which they approved of since I was happy to credit them under the photos. Then in early 2010, I saw this same guitar model on eBay with a starting bid of $3,000. I called the shop to see if they would hold the guitar before shipping it off to the winning bidder, so I could get the photos I needed. Cowtown told me, "No problem, bring a camera and take all the pictures you want." I also contacted Mr. King's office to inform them that this may be another guitar that was stolen from B.B.'s personal collection. I don't

Cell phone photos of 70th Birthday Lucille.

know if they followed up or not, but at least I felt I had done the right thing in letting them know. I called one final time to verify as I was prepared to drive to the store and I was told the guitar had already been shipped to the new owner, and even worse all of the pictures they posted on eBay were lost in a computer crash. So the only pictures I had were the ones I took on my cell phone at the store, until my research took me to the book *The Gibson 335 – Its History and Its Players* by Adrian Ingram (great book, by the way). You'll find a picture of the B.B. King 70th Birthday Commemorative Lucille on the upper right corner of page 83. This particular model of Lucille is considered an art guitar due to the incredible artistic effort that was lavished upon it and the limited quantity. I found a half page article on it from *Guitar Player* magazine from November 2002, when King was touring with his new favorite Lucille. Gibson presented this one to him as a birthday present as well. The article also revealed the name of Bruce J. Kunkel, the artist and master luthier behind the 70th Birthday Lucille and the B.B. King Tribute Lucille, who then owned and operated Kunkel Guitars; he was the driving force behind the 70th birthday edition. ♔

Before and after pictures of the B.B. King 70th Birthday Commemorative Lucille! Courtesy Dumitru Muradian

B.B. King 70th Birthday Commemorative Lucille closeup of pyrography. Courtesy Dumitru Muradian

B.B. King 70th Birthday Commemorative Lucille. Courtesy Dumitru Muradian

Chapter 16
BRUCE J. KUNKEL – MASTER LUTHIER

I tracked down Bruce Kunkel at his residence in East Stroudsburg, Pennsylvania, where he was building custom guitars, furniture, and other artistic endeavors. Kunkel comes from "a family of woodworkers," as he puts it best, but he started as a painter and that is something he excels at also! His father led the family into the woodworking trade, and Kunkel worked with his dad in Chester, New Jersey, in their woodworking school until he left to follow his own woodworking muse.

From 1992 until 2003, Kunkel was a Master Luthier/ Designer Creator of art guitars for Gibson. He reported directly to Mike McGuire, the Operations Manager at the Gibson Custom Shop at that time. He also worked with Rick Gembar, Gibson Custom Shop Manager since 1993 and now Operations Manager, who Kunkel stated, "brought out the best in me."

The story goes that McGuire was the one that brought the B.B. King 70th Birthday Commemorative Lucille project to Kunkel. It was also McGuire who had been contacted by a popular pyrographer named Dino Muradian (more on him later), who was based out of Los Angeles at that time. Kunkel sent Muradian the "white wood" (term used to refer to a guitar before any finish or other cosmetics have been applied) Lucille along with a photo of King to burn into the top of the body.

Upon its return to Nashville, Kunkel spent three to four weeks (while also over seeing regular guitar production at the Gibson factory) assembling and finishing the 70th Birthday Lucille. Kunkel wasn't certain why they produced this particular Lucille with f-holes (the first ever in the line of signature model Lucilles to be produced with this feature), but he stated that many of the unique ideas for this guitar came from brainstorming sessions including the song titles that were inlayed into the fingerboard. When asked how much he thought the guitar was worth, Kunkel said, "Only Christie's Auction house could put a price on it; I can't!"

To put aside the rumors, only one of the B.B. King 70th Birthday Commemorative Lucilles was created and presented to him at his big birthday party that same year by Gibson. So as the hunt for guitar knowledge and wisdom has continued, it finally led me to the artist that did the original artwork for the prototype 70th Birthday

Lucille that was given to B.B. by Gibson for his 70th Birthday – Dumitru (Dino) Muradian (who was also kind enough to supply me with his pictures of this model to use in this book).

I had the pleasure to take Kunkel and his lovely wife, Helen, with me to the B.B. King concert in Nashville in 2013, and we all had a great time sitting a few rows back from the stage right in the center of the Schermerhorn Symphony Center, along with my brother-in-law, Josh Puckett. Bruce Kunkel is a true artisan and continues to do incredible work for the Gibson Custom Shop in Nashville after moving back there in 2012. We frequently bump into each other at Nashville Guitar Shows now, and I understand there may be a book featuring all of his art guitars coming out soon! Kunkel is one of those unique people that actually puts a little of himself into every guitar he completes, and to my eye it shows! 👑

Bruce Kunkel holding a banjo that he handmade! Between 1992 and 2003, Kunkel was a Master Luthier/ Design Creator of Art Guitars in the Gibson Custom Shop. It is Kunkel who assembled and finished the B.B. King 70th Birthday Commemorative Lucille after Dino Muradian used pyrography to decorate the guitar. Image courtesy Bruce Kunkel

Chapter 17
DUMITRU (DINO) MURADIAN – ARTIST/PYROGRAPHER

So one late night in Las Vegas, I was doing more research on this book and hunting through my pile of reference books and searching the web. As I'm certain most of you know, you can find whatever you want or need on the web as long as you put the words in the correct order for the search engine to grab the website you are looking for and if you can determine what is real and what is fake.

As I was searching for information on the 70th Birthday Lucille, I finally came across an online wood carver's magazine with an article about the guy who actually did the pyrography on this particular Lucille. His name is Dumitru Muradian, or Dino as he is known to friends and most of the art world. So I did some more searches on him and found his personal website with a contact e-mail, assuming that he is either living in Seattle or in San Francisco as his bios had mentioned. I e-mailed him with various questions and asked if I could call him for a more in depth interview about this project.

To my surprise, the next day he had e-mailed me several pictures of the Lucille project, given me permission to use them in this book, and explained his story to me. Later on that same day, I got a call from Dino from his computer and to my surprise he was calling from Bucharest, Romania, where he currently lives and continues to ply his trade of pyrography, although now he does more violins, violas, cellos, and banjos than guitars.

Pyrography is the art of writing with fire, where the artist actually burns the images into wood, bone, cardboard, or other hard materials. This is not to be confused with wood burning, which most of us did in Boy Scouts and Girl Scouts here in the States. As Dino explained to me, "Here in Europe it's called pirogravure (French), in Romanian it's pirogravura, but pyrography is better I think, because in fact, no engraving is going on during the process. It's like photography - photographs, pyrography - pyrographs."

Dino has been carrying on this family tradition for over 50 years since his grandfather first taught him as a child. He now considers himself a "self-taught technician" rather than an artist since he

Dumitru (Dino) Muradian and B.B. King in his dressing room. Courtesy Dumitru Muradian

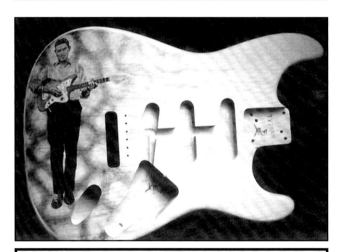

Pyrography for Jimmy Dean by Dino Muradian. Courtesy Dumitru Muradian

has had to innovate so many of his own custom tools and techniques. In 1993, he was living in the Seattle area and happened across a guitar magazine featuring Warmoth Custom Guitars and parts along with several blank natural wood guitar bodies. Dino began to visualize these guitar bodies as canvases to do artwork on, so he contacted them and did a Stratocaster body and neck covered in flowers.

Dino's life-long goal is to elevate pyrography to the level of fine art so that works of art like his and others could be displayed in art museums and galleries around the world. After speaking with him a number of times for these interviews, I believe if anyone can achieve this it is Dino. His work can easily be found on the web, in different magazines, and hanging around the necks of some rather prominent musicians like James Hetfield and B.B. King, including being the artist of Lucille #17!

The story goes that Dino had done a number of custom guitar projects for Fender, ESP, Jackson, Charvel, and even Tacoma (acoustic guitars), but he couldn't get Gibson to use him for a project. He also did the artwork on a Fender Stratocaster featuring a picture of the late Jimmy Dean for one of his birthdays. Then on a fateful day in 1995, the Gibson Custom Shop called up Dino and told him he needed to do pyrography on a Gibson Lucille for B.B. King's 70th Birthday present, and they need it in two weeks! Gibson sent him two pictures of B.B., one for the front and one for the back, but with the time limitations it

was agreed he would only do the one on the front so the Gibson Custom Shop would have enough time to finish the guitar and install the electronics before giving it to King. Once the unpainted/unfinished guitar was shipped to Dino in Seattle, he began his work with the final product taking him approximately 20 hours to complete. Then he boxed up the guitar and shipped it back to Memphis where the Custom Shop staff painted it and installed the electronics and finishing touches. The guitar was presented to B.B. on October 27, 1995, at his birthday bash at the Orpheum Theatre in downtown Memphis. The party included performances by Bobby Bland, Buddy Guy, Willie Nelson, Michael McDonald, Boz Scaggs, Isaac Hayes, Jeff Healey, Keb' Mo', Rufus Thomas, and Slash. Northwest Airlines had a DC-9-30 specially painted with "Lucille" and "Happy Birthday B.B. King" on it. B.B. autographed the jet as well! ♛

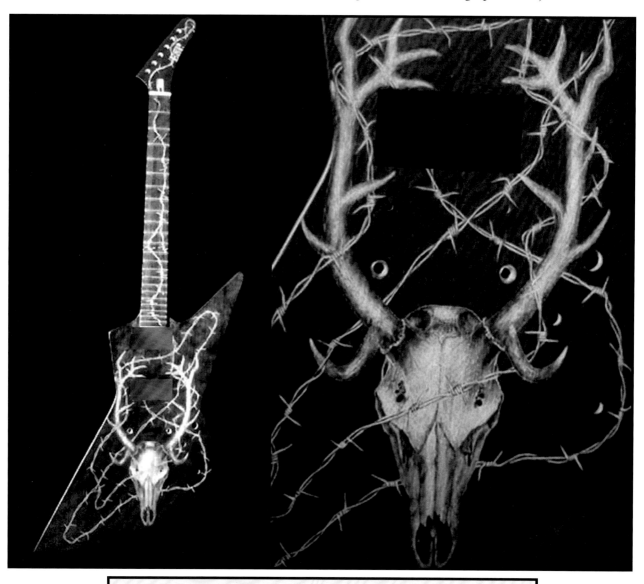

Pyrography for James Hetfield by Dumitru Muradian. Courtesy Dumitru Muradian

Chapter 18
MIKE MCGUIRE – GIBSON CUSTOM SHOP

Finding Bruce Kunkel led me to his close friend and one time boss, Mike McGuire, who was with Gibson since October of 1993, and retired as the Operations Manager of the Gibson Custom Shop in Nashville, Tennessee in 2012.

Mike related his first meeting with B.B. in California at a recording session with his friend, Larry Carlton, for his *Friends* album in 1983. Carlton had invited King mistakenly thinking he was Albert King and thought they would play "Hideway" on his new album. To his surprise, B.B. didn't know the song at all so they ended up doing "Blues for TJ" instead. McGuire was also put in charge of adjusting the volume on B.B.'s amp as the tracks were being laid down. McGuire has also distinguished himself in the guitar industry by launching the Valley Art Guitar Company with Duke Miller and Al Carness around 1969/70. Per McGuire, "We sold off the company to Samick around 1991."

He started his extensive career with Gibson in October of 1993, and was involved in Gibson's incredible Custom Shop endeavors up until his retirement. When asked what his involvement had been with the Lucille models, he said, "I [was] involved with every single model since 1993, especially all of the limited runs." In a one-on-one interview at the Gibson Custom Shop in Nashville, McGuire said that a number of "mules" were created over the years for B.B. to approve any time there were changes or updates to the models. As he explained to me, "mules" were rough prototype examples of the guitars that were designed to be changed and updated depending on what the artist specified! The same method was

Mike McGuire holding a Gibson Custom Shop Byrdland at his retirement party in August 2012. McGuire was the Gibson Custom Shop Operations Manager and was involved in almost every guitar out of the Custom Shop, including all of B.B. King's limited edition runs.

used during the launch of the Little Lucille, Super Lucille, 80th Birthday Lucille, Revised Standard Lucille (which came after the 80th Edition model), and the Lucille Gem models in 2010 in their various colors. McGuire retired in August of 2012 after serving 20 years with Gibson Guitars! Rick Gembar assumed this position after McGuire's departure. ♛

Chapter 19
GIBSON B.B. KING TRIBUTE LUCILLE

Bruce Kunkel was uncertain when the Gibson B.B. King Tribute Lucille was created, but since the guitar was dedicated to King's "50th Anniversary in the Recording Industry," it would place the creation date at 1999 since his first record was released in 1949. Mike McGuire, former Operations Manager for the Gibson Custom shop stated, "Bruce is a true artist who is very talented and he proved it on the Tribute guitar!"

What separates this Lucille from others is that it was hand painted and was based off of a "template" that Kunkel used for all of his art guitars. "The top of the guitar had a mature picture of the artist, action figure in the left portion, right section was juvenile and the back was the archetypical portrait," Kunkel said. For the back of the "Tribute Lucille," David Schenk, Gibson staff photographer, went and took an action picture of B.B. King at one of his concerts.

Other models featured in the Art Guitar Series included: Chet Atkins, Les Paul, Elvis, Merle Travis, and the 20th Century Tribute (which included 135 images with 18 karat gold inlays in the fingerboard). For some time, these guitars were toured around the country in a trailer so that Gibson fans everywhere could see these works of art. Unfortunately, the trailer did not have environmental controls, and Kunkel last heard the Chet Atkins model had not fared well from the travels.

Much like the 70th Birthday Lucille, it would be hard to assign a value to this model since only one was created and it took three to four weeks to create it. Besides the great hand painted artist renderings on the front and back of the "Tribute Lucille," it also featured King's name custom inlayed vertically in the fingerboard, an inlayed crown in the first fret, engraved pickup covers, and the pickguard had the Gibson Custom Shop logo inlayed on it (and stamped on the back of the headstock). More than likely, this incredible guitar will end up in a museum to be viewed as the art work that it is and the 50 years (at that time) that King had spent in the recording industry. ♔

Bruce Kunkel showing the front and back of the Gibson B.B. King Tribute Lucille he created. Photo courtesy Bruce Kunkel

Chapter 20
MY LUCILLE LIES OVER THE OCEAN – IMPORTS

Although most consumers think of Epiphone guitars as a budget or student line of instruments provided by the Gibson Corporation, at one time they were actually a direct American-made competitor with their now parent company. All of this changed in the late 1950s as Epiphone fell on hard times due internal family issues and mismanagement; Gibson's General Manager, Ted McCarty bought the company in 1957. In 1970, the new owners of Gibson and Epiphone moved that company's instrument production to Japan to make the brand more competitive with other imported guitars that were flooding the U.S. market at that time. The Epiphone brand, except for some special and Master Built models, has remained the home of imported instruments ever since, usually copying Gibson designs and offering a more affordable price point! This was probably the reason that Gibson launched an Epiphone version of their already popular, and 17 years in production, B.B. King Lucille model in 1997.

Besides being an import from Korea (and eventually China), the actual Lucille design has stayed fairly true to its original Gibson sibling. The main variations are the obvious Epiphone-shaped headstock and logo on top of the headstock and the "E" logo for Epiphone designation on the pickguard (which many players remove to give more of a Gibson-look to the guitar). Instead of the standard pickguard attachment to the guitar body, like its cousins the 335, 345, and 355, the Epiphone model has followed the suite of the student model Gibsons by having a bent metal piece that attaches to the side of the body and a screw coming through the middle of the pickguard to maintain distance from the body of the guitar. All of the other features from the Gibson model are included, but at a more reasonable imported price. This model has only been offered in Ebony with no special colors or other unique models, and it continues to be offered today. An Epiphone hardcase is available, but it is not included in the purchase of the instrument.

Several musicians I have spoken with actually prefer this model to the Gibson mainly for its lighter weight and thinner neck, as many other Epiphone models feature. In the past decade, many guitar dealers consider the Epiphone guitars to be equal to or superior to their American-made brothers. Unfortunately, value-wise they don't command the same respect or increases in market value that the American versions do. Although Mr. King has not been pictured touring with the Epiphone Lucille, he did give it his official seal of approval! 👑

The Epiphone B.B. King Lucille is very similar in appearance to the Gibson version, as illustrated from Epiphone's 2002 full line catalog. The picture of B.B. King looking at the headstock makes you wonder if anyone told him about the Epiphone version before the photo shoot!

Chapter 21
GIBSON B.B. KING SUPER LUCILLE

B.B. King's actual 80th birthday was coming up in September of 2006, and production of the Lucille model had recently moved from the Gibson Custom Shop in Nashville, Tennessee, to the Gibson Custom Shop in Memphis, Tennessee, in late 2001. In preparation for this major event, the Gibson team came up with the plan to give Lucille a special treatment. This included the use of abalone inlays (instead of the standard mother of pearl) in the Gibson headstock logo, Lucille logo, and fingerboard markers, which have a stunning three-dimensional appearance. It also has a custom black sparkle paint job, never before offered on a Lucille, which has very fine metal flake and reflects stage lighting well. The finishing touch was the artist hand-signed pickguard by B.B. King. I am told from sources inside Gibson that getting the artist to personally sign each pickguard was more challenging than originally thought (due to his rigid tour and travel schedule), so this model, which was planned to run through

Gibson Super Lucille music store detail card.

B.B. KING SUPER LUCILLE

Gibson has dressed up B.B. King's Lucille, one of the most famous guitars in the world, with gold sparkles in the ebony finish and abalone fingerboard inlays. It still sports the original Lucille's special features, including a Vari-tone with bypass setting and a top with no soundholes, and B.B.'s signature of approval is right there on the pickguard.

B.B. King Super Lucille. Image courtesy Gibson Guitar Brands

his big birthday, was scraped for the more production-friendly 80th Birthday model. I asked Mike McGuire about this and he said, "It's always hard including artist signatures on guitars. The most difficult was Les Paul, not because he wasn't happy to do it but we had to take a pile of pickguards and sit in the audience of the Iridium and wait until he finished playing to get them signed!" The Gibson Custom Shop records reflect that only 67 of these were created and shipped.

There was a special run in 2003 where 17 of the Super Lucille's were further customized for the American Diabetes Association fundraiser. The 17 guitars represented the 17 million Americans living with the diabetes disease, Mr. King being one of them, at the time in 2003, and $500 from each guitar purchased went to the charity. The Neiman Marcus Lucilles, as they have been called since this was the exclusive store they were sold through, have several variations compared to their other "Super" counterparts. First off, a round sterling silver artist proof medallion was attached to the upper horn front of the guitar and one on the back of the headstock. Next, on a standard "Super" the pickguard was hand signed by King; on the Neiman Marcus version, the upper left portion of the body was signed. The 17 guitars also included a special leather-bound picture book showing B.B. signing the Lucille, and it also had the instructions to send the instrument back to Gibson so the signature would be properly sealed. Both the standard Super and the Neiman Marcus Super came with a Gibson Custom Shop-signed certificate of authenticity, but the 17 were hand numbered on the back of the headstock and on the certificate. The last MSRP, as reflected by the *Blue Book of Electric Guitars*, was $4,000 for the regular "Super" model while the 17 Diabetes Foundation Neiman Marcus Super Lucilles fetched a whopping $6,300 plus shipping. 👑

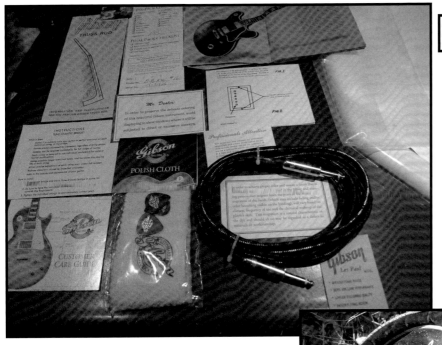

2003 Super Lucille case candy.
Image courtesy Gary York

Silver medallion on the back of the headstock. Image courtesy Gary York

Chapter 22
KING OF THE BLUES LIMITED EDITION GIBSON B.B. KING LUCILLE

In 2006, Gibson partnered with Guitar Center to create another special Gibson B.B. King Lucille model – this was the King of the Blues edition. Only 150 of these were made, and each one had an oval mother of pearl plaque attached to the back of the headstock, which reflected what number in the series it was. Standard features remained the same as the original Gibson Lucille, but other unique details included a special King of the Blues pickguard that had the "KOB" logo. Special brass volume and tone knobs with mother of pearl inserts were added on each of the guitars from the 150 piece run, plus they came with a certificate of authenticity signed by Rick Gembar from the Gibson Custom Shop and B.B. King. The neck on this limited edition guitar is slightly wider and fuller than most other Lucille models offered by Gibson.

I was told by a reputable source at the Gibson Custom Shop that this particular model sold out in two hours to the Guitar Center dealers across the country. Besides being eye-catching guitars, they really play and sound great, and I'm certain they were sold quickly once they arrived at the Guitar Center stores!

The unique engraved pickguard had me baffled at first, until I contacted a friend of mine at Guitar Center Corporate. It's easy to read the Guitar Center slogan for their semi-annual guitar competition, "King of the Blues." But I, and several other more knowledgeable guitar people than I, couldn't figure out what the "M" represented above the "KOB" script, whether it was for Guitarmageddon that was also involved with this project back in 2006 or something else. Then one of my friends from Guitar Center told me, "It isn't an 'M' at all; it is actually a crown, resting on top of the "King of the Blues" as a reflection upon B.B. King as its reigning king!" 👑

Gibson B.B. King Lucille - King of the Blues Limited Edition, 2006. Photography by Ted Vandell

Chapter 23
LITTLE LUCILLE GUITAR

Finding information about the Little Lucille poses a problem as Gibson has deleted most of their records, although there are a few forums that discuss all of the members in this family including the Nighthawk and Blueshawk. Supposedly this model was inspired by B.B. King's interest in the popular Gibson Blueshawk model (launched in 1996, discontinued in 2006, and briefly re-launched in 2010), which basically had a Les Paul-shaped single cutaway body without the carved top. The "Little Lucille" carried over many of the appointments its bigger sister did, per B.B.'s request. These included a TP-6 fine tuning bridge, cream binding on the body and fingerboard, diamond inlays, gold hardware, and the Vari-Tone selector. Like its cousin the Blueshawk, it retained the f-holes, mahogany body, rosewood fingerboard, and a pair of Blues 90 pickups. This guitar is easily identified by the "Little Lucille" in script on the body at the beginning of the fretboard and of course the B.B. King engraved truss rod cover on the headstock.

Although known for being a bit neck heavy, these are incredibly versatile player's pieces that get even more tonal variations with the remaining three position flip switch combined with the six position Vari-Tone! It was offered in Ebony, Wine Red, and Blues Burst colors and was discontinued from the Gibson line in 2004. B.B. was pictured with the Little Lucille when it was first launched, but I wasn't able to find any pictures of him actually performing on stage with one. Either way, these are great guitars and continue to appreciate in value much like the first generation Blueshawk and Nighthawk models. Even the hard cases for this model garner a hefty sum if you can find one! I procured my personal Little Lucille from a gentleman in Iowa that I tracked down on Craigslist. It's a great example and plays and sounds incredible, even though it is a bit neck heavy due to the lighter body from the semi-hollow body to accommodate the f-holes. 👑

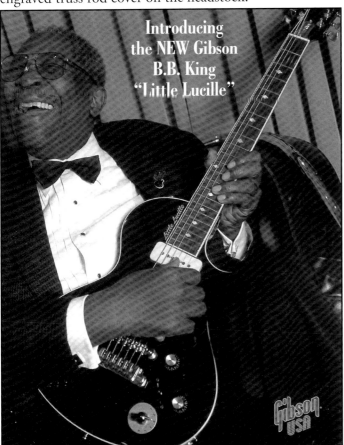

Introducing the NEW Gibson B.B. King "Little Lucille"

Gibson USA

This full page brochure of the Little Lucille indicates that B.B. King liked to play it! Fitted with traditional Lucille appointments, the Little Lucille looks tiny in King's hands.

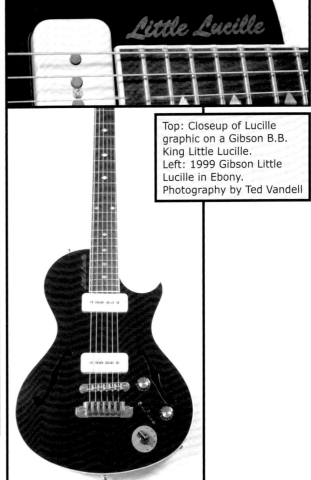

Little Lucille

Top: Closeup of Lucille graphic on a Gibson B.B. King Little Lucille.
Left: 1999 Gibson Little Lucille in Ebony.
Photography by Ted Vandell

Chapter 24
ALMOST MEETING B.B. KING

I moved to Las Vegas in the fall of 2001, to work with two television stations there (WB Las Vegas and Gold 33 at that time, now the CW Las Vegas and MYLVTV). After settling into the town and the stations, and moving my wife out from Missouri, I became close friends with several of my co-workers there whom I'm still friends with to this day. One of these was Jermaine Chappelle, who worked upstairs in our building in the accounting office with Meg, the business manager at that time. Jermaine also gave me the best advice I ever got while living in Las Vegas, as he knew I had moved straight out of rural Missouri to the big city. He said, "You see those big casinos down on the strip with all of those bright shining neon lights? They weren't built by winners!"

That pretty much broke the ice, so Jermaine and I started talking guitars, bands, music, and all of that good stuff and he tells me that he goes to church with (and is friends with) someone that works for B.B. King's Road Show office. He also informed me that Mr. King had lived in Vegas since the mid-1970s, and used this office and the city as his base camp. Upon Jermaine's urging, I went through my box of records and found two B.B. King records from the 1950s that had belonged to my father (my dad had signed them on the back so they wouldn't get stolen at frat parties). I was told to take the actual vinyl records out of the record covers, as Mr. King stated, "Sometimes things around here grow legs and walk away." So Jermaine gave them to his friend and we waited for King to come off the road from one of his tours; it was the spring of 2002. (He also encouraged me to buy a Gibson Lucille that King would sign, but having just moved there with my wife, our finances just wouldn't permit it at that time.)

Months passed and then we got word that they were signed and we would need to come down to the B.B. King Road Show office to collect them. The friend was Penny Morris, and she had been a valued staff member and friend of the King family for a long time. She came outside of the office and handed me an official B.B. King bag with my two record covers and other King goodies that included tour guitar picks, a Lucille pin, and some glossy color pictures of B.B. from his most recent tour. She was a very sweet and kind woman, and I won't ever forget what she and Jermaine did for me. Penny passed away in the summer of 2009, and the B.B. King Road Show office shut down for several weeks in her memory.

Now fast forward to 2007, and I still have the itch for a Gibson Lucille but just don't have the finances

Gibson B.B. King Lucille, with optional B.B. King signature fretboard inlay. Photography by Ted Vandell

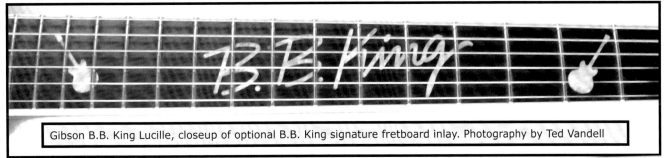

Gibson B.B. King Lucille, closeup of optional B.B. King signature fretboard inlay. Photography by Ted Vandell

for a brand new one. So I'm constantly scouring eBay, Craigslist, all of my local music stores, and many pawn shops. Finally one popped up on eBay with no reserve and upon closer inspection it was even located in Las Vegas. I contacted the seller and determined it was a pawn shop just blocks away from my home – score!

That same day I drove down to the EZ Pawn pawn shop to verify what the guitar is and the value. Upon seeing the prize, I knew she had to be mine even though she had some play marks and love taps on the back of the body, pick marks on the lower horn, and needed a good polishing, cleaning, and setup. This one even had the special order only feature of B.B. King's name inlayed in the fretboard in mother of pearl (MOP) with a MOP Lucille guitar inlayed on either side of his name as well (B.B. started playing a Lucille with his name inlayed in the fretboard back in the mid-'90s and continued to do so until Gibson gave him the 80th birthday model). I would later find out from Dennis Chandler that although King loved the look of these inlayed fretboards, "He didn't like the script inlayed B.B. name since it threw him off when he was playing." This was the first Lucille I ever purchased and from the marks and unique inlay, I

wondered if it had once belonged to King and was given away as a gift to a friend or fellow musician at some point. I went so far as contacting B.B.'s staff at the B.B. King Road Show office, George Gruhn (Owner of Gruhn Guitars in Nashville, Tennessee), *Vintage Guitar* magazine, and Gibson Corporation. The article on this one appears in Gruhn's column in *Vintage Guitar* in March of 2009.

All I determined in the end was that five of these were created in 2001, and all of them were sent to "a Gibson endorsed artist." From Gibson's records, they could not determine which artist this was or even where the guitars where shipped. Mr. King's staff believes it might have been a promotional guitar that they gave away back in 2001, which B.B. still frequently does for charities and causes to this day. From the pick marks on the top of the guitar and the higher than normal buckle rash on the back of the guitar, the play wear seemed very similar to another instrument that I briefly owned more than a year later. Either way I was told to keep it, play it, and enjoy it, and I certainly have over the years – plus it has a nice story and an article with it! 👑

Chapter 25
LUCILLE BECOMES A PAWN SHOP PRIZE

I'm not ashamed to say I'm a fan and frequenter of pawn shops all over the country, long before the *Pawn Stars* show brought them to the celebrity status they have achieved today. It seems that pawn shops have intrigued me since I was a young teenager back in Cape Girardeau, Missouri, and I would wander up to the local pawn shop that was downtown and right across from where I took guitar lessons since I was five years old - Key's Music Store.

After moving to Las Vegas in 2001, I found that the local music stores didn't carry as much vintage and used music equipment as I was used to, so the logical step was to start hitting the many pawn shops sprinkled all over town. I finally found the ones that bought, sold, and loaned money against music gear more than other items, so I had my usual stops every week and became friends with many of the staff at these shops. Besides getting calls when guitars and amps were falling out of hock, the pawn shops also used my expertise on gear values and in return would give me good deals on things I bought for helping – which I still do to this day.

During the ten years of making Las Vegas our home, I bought a lot of music gear, especially from a few of these shops, and as mentioned earlier, my first Lucille. In September of 2009, one of my buddies at a shop, Chaz Starr (he is now a pawn broker at Gold & Silver Pawnshop, which does the *Pawn Stars* TV show), called to let me know that another Gibson Lucille was coming out and would I like to see and possibly buy her before she hit the floor for the general public. What really caught my attention was that he said instead of the standard Lucille logo on the headstock it had a big "80" inlayed there. This piqued my interest, as I had never even heard of an 80th Birthday Lucille up until this moment.

Upon arriving at the pawn shop the next day, Chaz brought out the guitar in question. The case was beaten and torn and the guitar itself was covered in dirt, grime, sweat, and had plenty of scratches and nicks including on the

B.B. King's 80th Birthday Gibson Lucille Prototype #1.
Photography by Ted Vandell

metal pickguard (which had pick scratches all the way through the middle of the etching). My schooling on Gibson Lucille models had only begun a few years earlier, so I really didn't know what I was holding until I flipped over the guitar and saw "Prototype #1" stamped in white ink at the top of the headstock. I knew from reading books and from handling a few prototype guitars at NAMM (National Association of Music Merchants event held twice a year) shows over the years that if this was real and not a fake, then it should be the first guitar of this model line to be created and that in theory, B.B. King would have played it for at least five minutes to approve its production. I made a half-hearted attempt to get Chaz to budge on the price, but we both knew I was going to buy it anyway. I walked out of that Las Vegas pawn shop with a used and abused Gibson 80th Birthday Lucille for $2,161.99, which is the most I had ever paid for a guitar in my life (up until this point), and thus began my journey.

After taking her home, I began my usual regiment by cutting off the old strings, polishing off all of the dirt and grime, and setting up the action and truss rod to suit me; the guitar played and sounded like it had a soul of its own! 👑

Engraved pickguard - B.B. King's 80th Birthday Gibson Lucille Prototype #1. Photography by Ted Vandell

Engraved pickup covers and pickguard - B.B. King's 80th Birthday Gibson Lucille Prototype #1. Photography by Ted Vandell

Front of headstock - B.B. King's 80th Birthday Gibson Lucille Prototype #1. Photography by Ted Vandell

Chapter 26
LUCILLE – THE PLOT THICKENS

For the next two and a half months, I contacted every resource in the guitar biz that I could trying to find out if King ever held or approved this guitar – these resources included the Gibson Guitar Factory Representative Bob Burns (I e-mailed or called him almost every week with questions), Walter Carter (guitar book author/music store owner), Lee Diskin (Guitar Center), Wally Marx Jr. (author of *Gibson Amplifiers 1933-2008: 75 Years of the Gold Tone*), Joe Lowes (long time family friend and guitar collector), Josh Puckett (brother-in-law and guitar collector), and finally Zachary R. Fjestad (*Blue Book of Guitar Values*). Most of these contacts reached out to their friends that dealt in guitars trying to help me find every scrap of information possible! I pooled my information from all of these people and my nightly hunts on the web as I would vary my searches, word patterns, and search engines to find

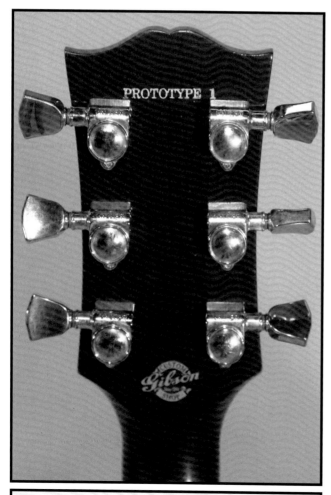

B.B. King's 80th Birthday Gibson Lucille closeup of Prototype #1 stamp. Photography by Ted Vandell

more facts. I had finally given up hope and resigned myself to just owning a cool Lucille that was worth more than what I gave for it and had more mojo than any guitar I had ever owned.

Then, on Tuesday, November 10, I got a phone call out of the blue from Pat Foley, Gibson Artist Relations, and he tells me I have a Gibson Lucille – which I explained to him, "Yes thank you, I have a few others; do you have any other information for me?" Then he said, "No you don't understand, you have B.B. King's personal Lucille that was stolen from him and he would really like it back – what's it going to take?" Foley went on to say, "Gibson gave this guitar to B.B. for his 80th birthday in L.A. and it means so much to him. We tried to create another just like her, but it just wasn't the same for the old man [affectionate term Gibson uses for King]." Pat said that they assumed the guitar had been stolen and sold off to Japan where many celebrity and custom one-off guitars ended up in private collections. He asked, "Where is the guitar at now?" This seemed like an odd question since it was obviously in my guitar room here at my home in Las Vegas with my other guitars, but I later learned there had been several instances like this in the past where people were trying to scam Gibson or Mr. King. Foley told me, "You're the only honest man in Las Vegas!" which I also thought was kind of funny since I had many honest friends in this city, but everyone outside of the town perceives it as Sin City - just the same, Pat meant it as a compliment to my coming forward with B.B.'s guitar.

After the great chat with Foley, I kind of felt like I was in a Charles Dickens story as I had been under radio silence for two and a half months researching this guitar and now everybody was coming out of the woodwork contacting me! The same day, my next call was from Tina France, Traveling Road Manager for B.B. King. She called to verify what I had and to talk to me one-on-one on behalf of King. She was very nice and we exchanged a number of calls, texts, and e-mails, even sharing pictures of her dog, Paris, and my daughter, Taylor. Next LaVerne Toney, Vice President of the B.B. King Road Show, who is based out of King's office in Las Vegas, contacted me. We had

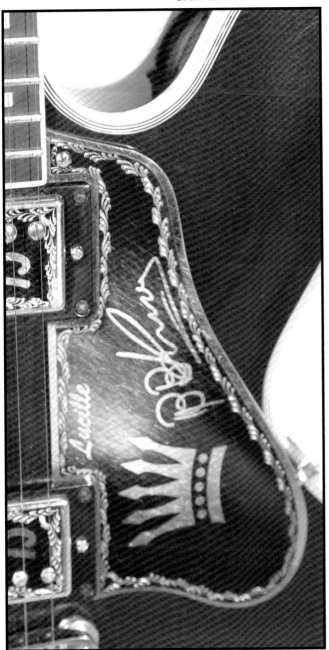

Engraved pickguard - B.B. King's 80th Birthday Gibson Lucille Prototype #1. Photography by Ted Vandell

spoken a number of times in the past as I was trying to get my pickguard for my other Lucille autographed and some posters for my guitar collecting buddies and me. She called up and said, "How much will it take to get Mr. King's guitar back?" At which point I told her "nothing," but I would like a replacement Gibson Lucille if possible since that is what I paid for at the pawn shop. So she ended up being the liaison between B.B. and me to set up the meeting and guitar exchange since King now wanted to meet me in person and thank me since I wouldn't accept any money for returning his Birthday Lucille.

The original meeting was set up for Wednesday, November 25, 2009, at 3 p.m. at the Road Show office. Unfortunately, Pat Foley from the Gibson Corporation, wasn't able to secure a Lucille shipped out from the Memphis, Tennessee factory in time for the meeting. So, King had LaVerne move the meeting to the Monday after Thanksgiving, keeping the 3 p.m. time and making it November 30, 2009. Ms. Toney was going to call me in the morning to rearrange the meeting again if the Lucille did not arrive, but we were on course for that day. ♔

Chapter 27
THE B.B. KING MEETING

The waiting game and sheer excitement were starting to wear me down. I told my wife the night before the exchange that whether Gibson came through with a Lucille for me or not, I was going to return Mr. King's Birthday Lucille to him because it was the right thing to do. She was very supportive of my decision and agreed with me. Ever since the call on November 10 from Gibson and B.B.'s staff, I told every guitar-collecting friend and family member that was willing to listen about the story – and most tolerated it pretty well.

Finally on November 30, it looked like everything was a go for the guitar exchange. My buddy, Steve Schiff, works over at the ABC affiliate in Las Vegas and the station was very interested in an exclusive on the story, but B.B. didn't want video cameras, reporters, and lights involved in this since he is so often in the public eye and really enjoys his down time more when he is off the road. He did allow me to bring my own still photographer, so I brought Ted Vandell, a co-worker from the TV station, with me.

We arrived at the Road Show office ten or fifteen minutes before the designated time, and I had the Prototype #1 Lucille in its original case with me, and I was handling it like the sacred lost treasure it was. Britney, the receptionist and LaVerne's daughter-in-law, told us B.B. hadn't arrived yet so we just milled around the foyer looking at many of the cool pictures of King with Elvis, presidents, his band, Stevie Ray Vaughn, and everybody who is anybody in the music world.

At a few minutes past 3 p.m., I looked out the door and saw B.B. King himself ambling up to the front door with a Diet Coke in his hand. Once he entered the foyer he reached out to shake my hand saying, "Hi, I'm B.B.!" I'm certain I responded back at this time, but I was so star struck I have no idea what I said to Mr. King as his giant hands engulfed mine in a warm handshake! He also brought his traveling assistant with him, Myron Johnson, a very quiet gentleman who now acts as King's personal assistant and handles private and business matters. Everyone in the back office was ready for B.B.'s arrival, so once he stepped in the office, the doors opened and King

B.B. King and the author at the November 30, 2009 meeting. Photography by Ted Vandell

B.B. King asks the author to lift up the 80th Birthday Lucille for closer inspection. Photography by Ted Vandell

The author returns the 80th Birthday Gibson Lucille to its rightful owner: B.B. King! Photography by Ted Vandell

B.B. King inspects his returned 80th Birthday Lucille with the author, with LaVerne Toney and Myron Johnson in the background. Photography by Ted Vandell

The author shows B.B. King the guitar parts he found in the center pocket of the case and asks if they're his. Photography by Ted Vandell

B.B. King pictured with the box for the author's Lucille in the background. Photography by Ted Vandell

B.B. King holds his returned 80th Birthday Lucille in his office in Las Vegas. Photography by Ted Vandell

B.B. King smiling at the November 30th, 2009 meeting at his Las Vegas office. Photography by Ted Vandell

asked LaVerne and Britney to lead the way back to his private office in the back of the building.

My assumption was that B.B. would take the position of president (which is his title on his business card) and sit at the head of his desk, but instead he sat down inches from me in front of the desk like he was a guest and the Birthday Lucille sat in the case between us. He cordially offered Ted and me a beverage, but I was personally trying to get my mind around this surreal event of being in the same room with one of my (and my father's) guitar idols and actually speaking to him one-on-one! After a few pleasantries, B.B. said, "Well let's take a look, do you mind opening up the case for me?" (Ted suggested to me weeks later that King probably didn't really believe that I had brought his special guitar until he laid his own eyes and hands on it.)

Leading up to the meeting, to help verify what they believed I currently had ownership of, I had already e-mailed pictures of the guitar to Gibson, Tina France, and LaVerne Toney. Plus, before King got off the last leg of his tour, he asked his assistant if I could bring the guitar by the office for her to inspect in person and see if she thought it was the real deal or not. Upon my opening the guitar case, King took one glance down and said, "That's her!" as a smile spread across his face. He then asked me if I would mind getting her out of the case for him since his back was causing him a lot of pain. After examining it for a few minutes in his lap, I asked him if the guitar strap and other guitar parts inside the case were his as well; this included two extra TP-6 bridges, two tune-o-matic bridges (all wrapped in tissues in plastic bags), and a worn Peavey guitar strap that smelled heavily of Angel cologne by Thierry Mugler (his favorite, LaVerne later told me) with strap locks attached. I had left everything intact just as when I had bought it from the pawn shop for some reason, except for the cleaning and replacement of the strings. King said, "Yep, it's all mine; that's just how it was in my case in my house." After that, he told Myron, "Let's put this one away and take a look at your new Lucille." I was like a kid at Christmas time as LaVerne brought over the Gibson Custom Shop box and we began opening it to release the Gibson case and Lucille from her cardboard confines. B.B. held it first when we got it out of the case, looked it over, and then handed it to me. He asked LaVerne to get some of his personal guitar picks and gave me

B.B. King and the author shaking hands after returning his 80th Birthday Lucille. Photography by Ted Vandell

three of his autographed picks to try the guitar out with. It had that new guitar smell and was so shiny and new, and King told me how proud he was of the Lucille Gibson makes for him and he hoped I liked her, too, which of course I did.

After that, we just sat in his office and talked for a while and didn't even notice anyone else in the room with us. I told Mr. King how nice it was that he played at Bo Diddley's funeral the year before since I was a fan of him as well. King stated how they didn't even mention his name, Buddy Guy's, or John Mayer's, and that "blues players get slighted a lot."

After the women had left the office, Mr. King looked around the office and leaned over to me and said," Now that the women folks are gone, if Lucille had a vagina I would [expletive] her." We all had a great laugh as King seemed just as young and vital as I'm certain he was in his younger days. I asked B.B. about the *B.B. King Treasures* book, and Mr. King said, "I never read it and wasn't involved in the writing [of] this one." But he said he was very involved with the writing of *Blues All Around Me*, a great book co-authored by David Ritz. I told him that I planned to buy a copy and read it, and he said they had some copies lying around the office and that he would have his assistant find me one and some t-shirts, too.

I asked Mr. King if Gibson put real diamonds in the crown on the headstock for him since it was for his birthday. King said (in his booming almost laughing voice), "No, Gibson wouldn't put real diamonds in there for me," but personally I still wonder if they were real. B.B. did go on to say that he tried out several of the 80th Birthday Lucilles and then chose this one above all of the others because of how it played and sounded. And that they built it to his exact specifications!

As Ted Vandell brought his professional still camera and started taking pictures, Mr. King was so gracious he told me to take all of the pictures I wanted and to do whatever I wanted with them, with magazines or whatever. Honestly, I was so focused on listening to and speaking with Mr. King I never noticed Ted taking pictures until we were leaving the office. B.B. did ask for a copy of the picture that was taken that day showing me and him together with his returned Lucille. My running joke with his staff at the B.B. King Road Show office (and my friends) is that the picture is probably hanging in his bathroom there and every time he goes in he wonders who the funny-looking guy with the flat top and goatee is!

As we were discussing the theft of his guitar, B.B. said that one of his own people had stolen it right out of his home while he was upstairs and that man took

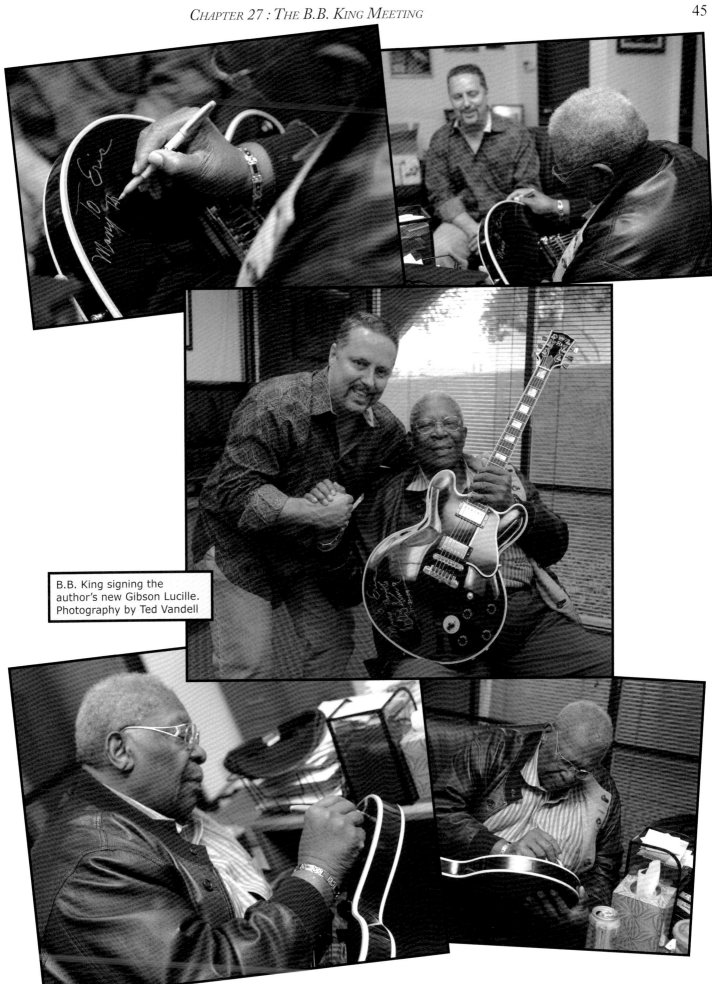

B.B. King signing the author's new Gibson Lucille.
Photography by Ted Vandell

the case and all. He said that the person who stole it had already been fired earlier that year for drugs, as that is one thing he will not tolerate in his band because people don't say such and such got busted for drugs; it's "one of B.B. King's band members was arrested for drugs," and he doesn't want that kind of press. The suspected man was stopped as they were returning from Canada and he had a cigar box that also had marijuana seeds in it. Once they returned to Las Vegas, the band member in question was fired. Mr. King asked me to give his assistant LaVerne the name of the pawn shop, the location, and phone number, which I was happy to do. King also said that he wouldn't be prosecuting the man and that he hoped he had his act cleaned up now. But, he wanted to call the pawn shop so that if he came in again they could tell him, "She is back where she belongs [meaning Lucille], and he [B.B. King] knows who did it." I thought that was very old school, but I also thought it was incredibly kind as Mr. King obviously cherished this guitar, but he also didn't want to make it harder on this man who had stolen from him and actually hoped he had cleaned up his act.

The statement that will stick with me for the rest of my life from this meeting was towards the end of the conversation as Mr. King leaned in and said," I gotta get back on the road and make some money." In reflection, I don't think it's about the money, but more about the road calling him back as his one true home.

I knew that Mr. King took time out of his busy schedule just to meet with me, and I didn't want to waste his time as he was in the middle of recording sessions with Joe Bonamassa in Las Vegas for a new CD that would eventually be released. I thanked Mr. King for his generosity and time and told him that Ted and I should probably let him get back to business matters and I shook his hand again.

I didn't realize it until after our meeting, but the guitar pictured with B.B. on his 80th Birthday CD and *One Kind Favor* was the guitar I returned. It is also the guitar I saw him perform with at the Ryman in Nashville in 2011, and the one he used to perform for President Obama at the White House on February 21, 2012.

As we were leaving, he told me how much he liked the vibrant shirt I was wearing. I didn't realize how much it was like many of the shirts and sports coats he wore at concerts he played. I explained to him that my wife had picked it out just for this meeting. As Ted and I walked down the hallway leaving his office, Mr. King was waving goodbye and said, "God Bless you, young man, and thank you." And I think He definitely has with this moment in time and with my family and friends. ♔

Chapter 28
ANTHONY BRAGG – GIBSON CUSTOM SHOP STAFF

I met Anthony Bragg not long after I moved to Nashville, Tennessee, in the spring of 2011. I was searching Craigslist (as I frequently do) and found a Gibson Les Paul-shaped guitar table that was priced right, so Anthony and I haggled and then met at a Home Depot parking lot and I paid what he was asking in the first place, which was still a deal. Before he moved to Austin, Texas, to be closer to family, he also sold me a pair of vintage '70s Thomas Organ Cry Baby Wah pedals that are shown in this book as well.

Bragg not only worked on tooling and machining for numerous Lucille models during his tenure at Gibson, but he was also the man that machined the unique brass pickguard and metal truss rod covers for the 81st and 82nd 80th Lucilles that were created. What was different about the headstock veneers on the 80th Birthday models was, "Each veneer was countersunk with holes to receive the jewels prior to having them glued to the headstock of the instruments," Bragg said, "After the topcoat and buff, then the instruments returned to my shop to have the jewels installed." He went on to say, "We painstakingly retouched all of the countersunk holes to the proper size and set the jewels in with glue that we created with nitrocellulose lacquer top coat." The jewels used in the headstock were purchased from a local shop in Nashville.

Anthony now resides in Austin, Texas, close to his

Anthony Bragg while working at the Gibson Custom Shop. Courtesy Anthony Bragg

brother and continues to work in the music industry there. He worked briefly for Teye Guitars in Austin and is now considering launching his own line of guitars and amps. I have been promised that I will get to play and review some of the early prototypes when they rollout! 👑

Chapter 29
GIBSON B.B. KING COMMEMORATIVE ES-355 LUCILLE THE 80TH BIRTHDAY EDITION

The official designation for this guitar is the B.B. King Commemorative ES-355 "Lucille," but most collectors just know it as the 80th Birthday Lucille since that is the reason why it was created, to honor King's birthday. Gibson, from their literature and customer service contacts, states that 80 Gibson B.B. King Lucille 80th Birthday guitars were created in celebration of Mr. King's 80th birthday in 2005 (the limited edition was released in 2006). Counting Prototype #1, which belongs to B.B., there are actually 82 of the 80th Birthday Lucilles documented as existing. It is also rumored that one or two others may have been created or kept by Gibson employees, but this can't be substantiated or denied at this writing.

I found out about Prototype #2 in the fall of 2012 when a collector from Chicago, Eric Ewen, e-mailed me that he had recently bought a Lucille from Willie King, B.B.'s son, who also lived in Chicago. At first I thought it was just a clever forgery and that Ewen might have been taken in by a copy. But, after doing some research and contacting Pat Foley at Gibson, I was told that Gibson more than likely created a few prototypes for King to choose from and that the one he chose was stamped #1 and the other #2 and that he took them both and gave one to his son – which was eventually sold.

Of the total 80 guitars that were created for the general public, 44 of these were ear marked for the United States market while the other 36 were sold internationally. Each guitar has a stamped ink serial number at the back of the headstock, in the usual Gibson location, and then underneath that is a hand written X of 80 to indicate the number it was in the series. The Gibson Custom Shop logo is also stamped at the bottom of the back of the headstock where the headstock and neck begin to join. Each of these guitars left the Gibson factory with two signed certificates: one that verified that it commemorated B.B. King's 80th birthday and was signed by King; the second one was from the Gibson Custom Shop, and both verified the number of the guitar and its serial number.

What separates this model from the other Gibson Lucilles is the following: unique black pearl finish (only

offered on this model), 80th Birthday headstock veneer with cubic zirconium jewels in the headstock, Gibson-inscribed metal truss rod cover, B.B. King signature and crown inscribed on the metal pickguard, B.B.'s initials engraved in each pickup cover, special UFO-shaped volume and tone knobs with mother of pearl inserts in the middle of each, and a personally signed certificate of authenticity included with each guitar. These were only sold in 2006, and from what I was told they sold out quickly, as buyers were encouraged to pre-order once the word got out about their creation from Gibson. They are a rare find and play and sound incredible. 👑

Front of headstock - B.B. King's 80th Birthday Gibson Lucille Prototype #1. Photography by Ted Vandell

B.B. KING CUSTOM LUCILLE

Gibson introduced B.B. King's signature model in 1980 with two variations: a Standard and a Custom. The standard had chrome hardware and relatively simple appointments. The Custom, with gold hardware and higher appointments, became more popular and evolved into the "Lucille" that we associate with today - the Standard version was discontinued in 1985. Since 1980, very little has changed from the Lucille aside from a few minor model name tweaks. In 2007, the headstock was redesigned with a new B.B. King custom logo, gold truss rod cover inscribed with "Lucille", and graphics without the Gibson logo. This is the model B.B. King performs with today and it continues to hold a spot in Gibson's standard production line-up of guitars. Images courtesy Gibson Guitar Brands

B.B. KING LUCILLE GEM SERIES

While nearly everyone associates B.B. King with his black-finished Lucille, other colors of his famed guitar exist as well. The Gem Series probably steers furthest from the traditional Ebony finish, but it was done tastefully and gave collectors another option in their B.B. King collection. In late 2010, Gibson created a line of Lucilles exclusively through Musician's Friend's Private Reserve Collection. Five different colors were offered in very limited quantities of 25 each. They included: Sapphire (blue), Ruby (red), Emerald (green), Diamond (white), and Amethyst (purple). It turns out that B.B. King's favorite colors were Emerald and Diamond, which were also the public's favorite in terms of sales. MSRP on the Gem Series was $5,175 each with a selling price of $3,699 after standard discounting. Images courtesy Gibson Guitar Brands.

B.B. KING WITH LUCILLE INLAID ON FINGERBOARD

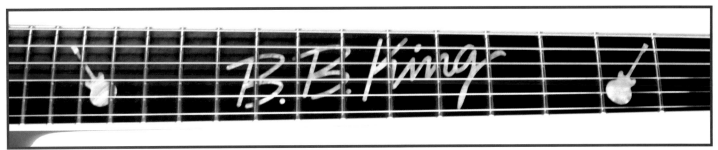

In the mid-1990s, B.B. King started playing a Lucille with his name inlaid on the fingerboard in mother-of-pearl. Since this wasn't standard equipment on the production Lucille, Gibson began offering a custom-order version with his name inlaid into the fingerboard in 2002. This special order option was offered through 2004, and was discontinued as Gibson was developing a new Lucille for his 80th birthday model, which King began playing exclusively. Production was limited on the inlaid fingerboard Lucilles and they command a premium over the production model. Images courtesy Gibson Guitar Brands and Ted Vandell

In this 1996 concert picture, you can clearly see King playing a Lucille with his name inlaid into the fingerboard. This became available as an alternative to the Custom Lucille model between 2002 and 2004. Image courtesy Jerry Adler

B.B. KING SUPER LUCILLE

In preparation for B.B. King's 80th birthday celebration, Gibson decided to give the Lucille a special treatment in 2002. This limited edition guitar featured abalone inlays on the fingerboard, headstock, and in the Lucille logo, a black sparkle paint job, and a hand-signed pickguard by B.B. King himself. A total of 67 of these were produced at a retail price of $4,000. In 2004, Gibson produced an additional 17 Super Lucilles as Artist Proofs to raise money for the Diabetes Foundation, and they were sold exclusively through Neiman Marcus. Seventeen of these were produced to represent the 17 million Americans living with diabetes at the time. Images courtesy Gibson Guitar Brands

Shown on stage in 2003, B.B. King is playing one of the limited edition Super Lucilles. However, note that the pickguard doesn't have B.B. King's hand-signed autograph. Many owners of the Super Lucille (including King) removed the pickguard and replaced it with a regular Lucille pickguard to prevent the signature from getting ruined! Image courtesy Jerry Adler

B.B. KING 80TH BIRTHDAY LUCILLE

The 80th Birthday limited edition of the Lucille represents the most expensive Lucille produced to date. At a retail price of $9,840 in 2006, this was double the price of any other Lucille offered in the mid-2000s. The 80th Birthday Lucille was also produced in combination with B.B. King & Friends' *80* album, which was a birthday tribute to King. The headstock design and inlays match the artwork on the album! Other highlights include ornate appointments, a Black Pearl finish, and a certificate of authenticity. Of course, the 80th Birthday Lucille was produced in a limited quantity of 80 instruments - including prototype one that was owned by the author. Images courtesy Ted Vandell

B.B. KING "KING OF THE BLUES"

Gibson partnered with Guitar Center in 2006 to create another limited edition B.B. King Lucille to be sold exclusively in their stores. The "King of the Blues" moniker was chosen to pay tribute to King's status as the king of the blues genre of music. It is similar to the production Lucille with notable changes including a special King of the Blues pickguard, brass volume and tone knobs with mother of pearl inserts, a slightly wider neck, and a certificate of authenticity signed by Rick Gembar of the Gibson Custom Shop and B.B. King. Only 150 of these limited editions were produced and they reportedly sold out in two hours to Guitar Center dealers across the country! While at first glance the pickguard looks like it has an "M" above the King of the Blues script, it is actually a crown - another subtle, yet appropriate appointment for the king! Images courtesy Ted Vandell

LITTLE LUCILLE GUITAR

The Little Lucille is the one B.B. King guitar model that is totally different than any others as it is not based on an ES-335. The Little Lucille traces its origins to the Gibson Blueshawk/Nighthawk series of guitars that were popular in the mid-1990s. The Little Lucille takes the overall shape and feel of the guitar, but with King's unique appointments that grace most of the Lucilles including a TP-6 fine tuning bridge, cream body and fingerboard binding, diamond inlays, gold hardware, and a Vari-Tone selector. It was only produced for five years between 1999 and 2004, but it has become quite collectible today even without a vintage status. Images courtesy Gibson Guitar Brands and Eric Dahl

EPIPHONE LUCILLE

For those who can't afford a top-of-the-line Gibson Lucille or are looking for something to take out on the road or play on stage, Gibson released a budget version of the Lucille through their Epiphone line in 1997. At a retail price slightly above $1,000, this guitar has a very attractive price point allowing almost anyone access to a Lucille. Produced overseas in Korea, and later in China, the Epiphone Lucille is very similar to the Gibson version. Aside from a slightly different pickguard design and Epiphone badging, these two guitars are nearly identical. B.B King has not been pictured touring with an Epiphone version; however, he has given it his seal of approval! Image courtesy Gibson Guitar Brands

A familiar sight: B.B. King and his beloved Lucille. Shown in concert circa 1996. Image courtesy Jerry Adler

Chapter 30
A LUCILLE BY ANY OTHER COLOR

Besides the creation of the original B.B. King Signature model Lucille, the 70th Birthday Lucille, the 80th Birthday Lucille, the King of the Blues Lucille, and the B.B. King Tribute ES-345, the craftsmen at the Gibson Custom Shop have still found time to create a number of one-off Lucilles just for King! Charlie Dennis has personally seen and restrung Blue, Red, and Blonde Lucilles over the years. He said, "B.B. would take one of these custom Lucilles on the road as a backup, and I would have all new strings on it and ready to go, but when he would break a string during the show he would just ask me for another string and fix it on stage himself." Part of this was due to fans and the general public only wanting to see B.B. with an original Ebony Lucille as he has always been seen with in the past. Charlie said, "When he took out the Blue Lucille or the Blonde one out, the fans didn't like it; they want to see him with the original Black one like they always do."

Robert Garland, B.B.'s amp and guitar guru, mentioned another special one-off Lucille that Gibson made for King for a Christmas present back in December of 2001. Garland stated, "The entire guitar was painted gold, and the Gibson staff had painted, on the front body of the guitar, 'Merry Christmas from your Friends at Gibson' and there was a big hand-painted Christmas tree on it, too." The Gold Christmas tree Lucille is rumored to only have been played out once on a TV Christmas special.

Limited Edition Gem Series Amethyst (Purple), Diamond (White), and Emerald (Green). Image courtesy Gibson Guitar Brands

Of King's 300-plus guitars, per Charlie Dennis, in his personal collection at this time – it would be impossible to know how many different colors and variations have been created for B.B. by Gibson without going through every single case in his collection!

B.B. King and Gibson are known supporters of many charities and what better way to help out a charity than with a custom made Lucille created in limited quantities and signed by the King. After the 9/11 tragedy, Gibson, King, and MCA records partnered with the United Way to create ten "hand-crafted, hand-painted, and signed" Lucilles for an online auction. This particular "Lucille" model was created in red and had a wreath painted on the front of the body. Over $30,000 dollars was raised for the September 11th fund.

In May of 2003, Gibson also teamed up with King to support the City of Hope National Medical Center. Nine "Limited Edition City of Hope Holiday Lucille Guitars" were autographed by B.B. and auctioned off for the charity that year. These were created on a blue painted Lucille with special "City of Hope" holiday

graphics on the front. Usually when these models are created, Gibson makes an extra one just for King to have as a memento, so it would be a fair assumption that ten of these were made in 2003.

The next Custom Shop Edition could just be a White Lucille. In the middle of June 2010, I was on the road for my day job and visiting two of my TV markets in one week. While waiting at an airport in Oklahoma City to fly to Des Moines, I got a call from Pat Foley. He was vacationing at the time in Napa Wine Country, but he wanted to let me know he did have a letter written up to verify the Lucille that B.B. signed and gave to me, plus an extra Lucille pickguard that I needed for one of my guitars. Pat also mentioned, "A promoter wants to do a limited run of 15 White Lucilles. If I can get B.B. to sign off on it, would you like to buy number 16." Of course my answer was yes, and that limited run ended up being the Gem Series of Lucilles that were released in late 2010. Pat has mentioned he would like me to be involved in future Lucille productions just as a consultant in the future, to help carry on B.B.'s legacy. ꝏ

Limited Edition Gem Series Ruby (Red) and Sapphire (Blue). Image courtesy Gibson Guitar Brands

Chapter 31
A GEM OF A B.B. KING LUCILLE

B.B. King pictured with the 2010 Limited Edition Gem Series Lucilles. Image courtesy Gibson Guitar Brands

As quoted from the online advertisements, "New Hues for the King of the Blues," this special series of Lucilles was introduced as part of Musician's Friend's Private Reserve. In the fall of 2010, I was notified by a Gibson Representative that they were creating a limited run of Lucilles that would be launched through Musician's Friend online and through their catalog. Apparently, B.B. agreed to let the Gibson Custom Shop create Lucille in colors that had never been offered to the public before, although Red and Blue have been offered but in different variations.

The Limited Edition Gem Series included Emerald (Green), Amethyst (Purple), Ruby (Red), Diamond (White), and Sapphire (Blue). Under the online advertisement, which pictured King laughing and surrounded by the guitars, the individual guitars were shown with the specific jewel they were named after. The offering was set to be only 50 in each color, and they were offered as a pre-order on Thursday, November 11, 2010, (they ended up only offering 25 in each color). The representative at Musician's Friend total me the guitars were set to arrive at their

warehouse on November 22 and would ship out within one to two days after that. It is noted that King's personal favorites from this run were the Emerald Green and the Diamond White, and he actually took the prototype guitars from the photo shoot home with him after the pictures were taken to promote them. Gibson also promised to provide B.B. one in each color for his personal collection once they were released.

The Diamond and Emerald colors were also the most popular choices with the public, per Musician's Friend. The MSRP for these models was $5,175 and Musician's Friend sold them exclusively online for $3,699. The MSRP for a standard Gibson Custom B.B. King Lucille was $4,449 at the same time and was sold online for $3,149, so it was basically a $550 increase for the different colors and extra goodies. Other unique extras with this Lucille included a certificate of authenticity booklet, which for the first time in Custom Shop and Memphis factory history was printed with a color matched artwork to the guitar it was sold with, i.e. the Emerald guitar got an Emerald book. On the cover of the certificate holder, there was a picture of B.B. King and his crown logo. The guitar package also came with a *The Best of B.B. King Christmas Collection* CD and a copy of his book, *The B.B. King Treasures*. The amazing part of this isn't just the creation and general release of the different colored Lucilles, but also that King allowed himself to be photographed with not one but all of the multi-colored Lucilles at once. Previously, a photo like this never would have been allowed since B.B. knows what the public expects from him in his clothes and in his color choice for Lucille. The standard Custom Shop and Epiphone Lucilles continued to be offered while these were being sold also.

The Musician's Friend representative that I spoke to stated that they were launching the model with "very limited quantities," but also if they sold well that the Gibson Custom Shop might increase the number of pieces. I also learned that there were on-going talks between Gibson and B.B. about the possibility of more color variations such as sparkle finishes in the future. Only time will tell what other flavors of Lucilles may be available.

I personally acquired the Diamond and Emerald models in this series and am very impressed with the craftsmanship of both. What struck me as odd, since I pre-ordered mine as soon as humanly possible, was that my Diamond (white) Lucille was #7 of the run while my Emerald (green) was #49 (Mr. King's office was surprised I got both of them so quick since he hadn't received any of his, except for the ones he acquired from the photo shoot.) I contacted my Musician's Friend representative and asked how the serial system had been worked with

Gibson, as it made sense to do, made White as one through twenty-five and on down the line in the colors. In his words, "There is no rhyme or reason on why Gibson numbered the guitars this way." From what he told me, this is very common when they produce Artist Special Edition guitars, and the serial numbers in this series in no way reflect the order in which they were made. It would seem logical that Gibson would do a serial number run like BBK0007D to signify the seventh in the Diamond series, but I don't think logic always applies in the serial number equation. Ultimately, there were to be 125 total Gem guitars created for this run, and with the popularity of it, there is already talk of what the next Lucille variation might be in the future. 👑

Chapter 32
THE KING GOES ACOUSTIC

Since he went electric back in 1948 by adding a pickup to his first Lucille, the Gibson L-30 guitar, B.B. has seldom been seen in public actually playing an acoustic guitar. There is a vintage picture of him holding his cousin Booker (Bukka) White's resonator guitar. His earliest guitars, Stellas, were also acoustics, but that was only because that was all he could afford at the time and all that was available to the public. It has been noted in the past, from several reliable sources, that King keeps several acoustics around his home just to play and practice when he is off the road. In 1994, B.B. King was pictured in an advertisement holding the Gibson L-00 "Blues King" to help introduce this model. The L-00 model was very similar to Robert Johnson's L-0 acoustic Gibson guitar that Johnson was pictured

with, in one of the few surviving photos of him. The L-00 originally came out in 1932, and featured a spruce top along with mahogany back and sides; it was discontinued in 1942, but was very popular in the '30s. Gibson reintroduced the L-00 (1936 Reissue in 1992 through 1996, and again from 1999 to 2002), and utilized B.B.'s blues influence to give the reproduction a more authentic feel for the public. When asked if he played this model or other acoustic guitars at home, on tour, or in the studio, King is quoted from the *Guitar Player Repair Guide* as stating, "I've got two or three of them around home (acoustic guitars). One is an old National with the tin body and a resonator." I'm certain he has accumulated more acoustics since that 1992 interview, but how many is anyone's guess, although I know Gibson was working on some custom acoustics for him at one time. ♔

Gibson L-00 acoustic guitar ad featuring B.B. King.

L-00 Vintage Sunburst. Image courtesy Gibson Guitar Brands

Chapter 33
LUCILLE – CITIES OF MANUFACTURE AND DATING

The original creation of the Gibson B.B. King Lucille signature models, including the prototypes, all started at the Gibson factory on Parsons Street in Kalamazoo, Michigan. Per Dennis Chandler, "The first run and prototypes of Lucille were all made in Kalamazoo," starting in 1980. The Nashville, Tennessee factory opened in 1974, but manufacturing of the Lucille did not move there until 1982, since the lower level and budget models were only made there in the beginning. Chandler said, "If there were any Kalamazoo models in 1982, the numbers were small. There were certainly a few during the transition." Another interesting point that Chandler brought up on dating and manufacturing was, "It is possible that some of the necks were attached to the bodies in Kalamazoo. Some of those could have been completed in Nashville although the serial numbers would indicate Kalamazoo!"

Since B.B.'s model was a custom-made signature model, it is logical to assume that the more seasoned craftsmen in the Kalamazoo factory would be the ones to build these.

As with most Gibsons, the serial number is the only real way to identify where the guitar was made. After the transition from the six digit serial number system to the eight digit system of identification in 1977, you were able to tell which factory a guitar was made in by the last three digits on the back of the headstock. Per the *Blue Book of Electric Guitars*, the pattern goes like this:

YDDDYPPP

YY is the production year

DDD is the day of the year

PPP is the plant designation or instrument rank.

Numbers ranging from 001 to 499 signify the manufacturing occurred in Kalamazoo, while 500-999 reflects a Nashville build. This system continued until 1989, even after the closing of the Kalamazoo factory in 1984. In 1989, Gibson opened the Bozeman, Montana factory to produce acoustic guitars. This left Nashville to solely focus on electrics, until 2001 when the Memphis factory opened to build electric archtops. When acoustic production began in Bozeman in 1989, Gibson reorganized

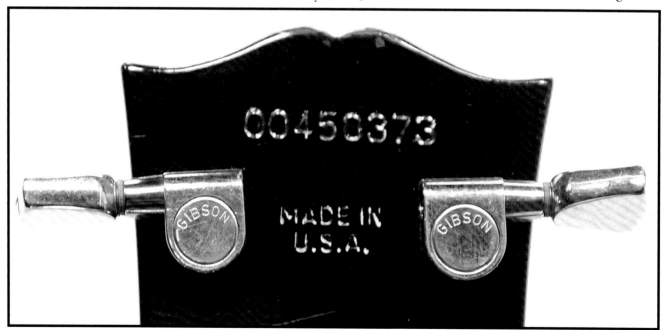

This serial number from a standard production Lucille utilizes Gibson's normal eight-digit serial number. Based on the serial number, this guitar was built on Valentine's Day (February 14) in 2000. Since 1977, Gibson has used this system to date their guitars where the first and fifth digits indicate the last two digits of the year and the second, third, and fourth digits indicate the day of the year based on the Julian calendar. On this guitar "0" and "0" tell us 2000 for the year and "045" tells us the 45th day of 2000, or February 14. Image courtesy Eric Dahl/Marc Kordalski

the production ranking numbers to reflect the new factories, especially since Kalamazoo had closed five years earlier leaving numbers 001-499 unused. Acoustic guitars built in Bozeman begin each day at 001 and run consecutively up to 299 (Bozeman never produces more than 300 instruments a day). Nashville guitars start at 300 and run consecutively up to 999. This system remained in place until 2005, when Nashville began producing or approaching production of more than 700 guitars per day.

Beginning in July 2005, Nashville adopted a new system where a "batch" number was added to give a total of nine digits in the serial number. This allowed production to go past 700 instruments without duplicating numbers. This batch number is now the sixth digit, while all the others remain the same. It should be noted that only Nashville utilizes the new nine-digit serialization system – Bozeman and Memphis do not, so Lucilles should still have an eight-digit serial number. Also, Gibson clarified things greatly in circa 2011 by physically stamping "Made in 2011" for guitars produced that year. On limited edition Lucilles, Gibson used unique serialization systems to identify these guitars, which is common in the Gibson Custom Shop. For instance, the B.B. King Lucille Gem Series have a "BBK" prefix followed by four digits that are simply a rolling production number – there is no dating information in the serial number!

Since Epiphone Lucilles are produced overseas, they follow Epiphone's serialization system, which is usually a letter prefix (to identify what country/factory the guitar was produced in) followed by a series of numbers that usually has a key to date the instrument. In recap, Lucille was launched and refined in Kalamazoo from 1980 until 1982, then in 1982, the Nashville factory started manufacturing them, and finally in 2001, production moved to Memphis, Tennessee, where all custom and standard Gibson Lucille models continue to be produced to this day. This of course excludes the Epiphone models, which are made primarily in Korea and China.

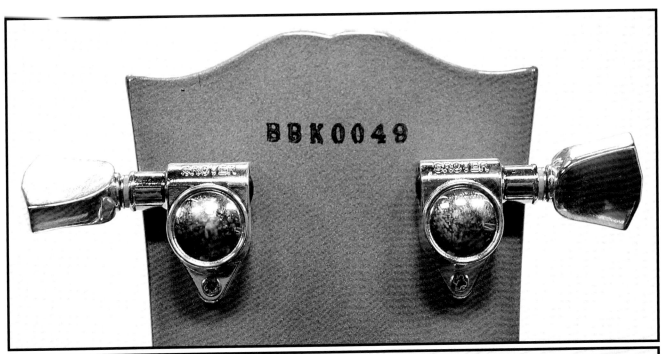

On Custom Shop models and limited editions, Gibson often uses a unique serialization system for each model to help identify them. For the B.B. King Gem Lucilles, Gibson utilized a "BBK" prefix followed by four digits that were simply a chronological number sequence. Unfortunately, on serial numbers like this there isn't any year identification so a person would have to know when it was produced to actually date it. Image courtesy Eric Dahl/Marc Kordalski

Chapter 34
LUCILLE CAN'T BE FAKED?

The nice thing about having lots of great friends at guitar shops and pawn shops around the country is you get some fun calls on pricing and verification for incredible pieces, and you also run across a number of counterfeit guitars. (My most recent call was from a gentleman in Kingman, Arizona, who had inherited Hank Williams, Sr.'s childhood guitar amp from his uncle).

Everyone remembers the big lawsuit between Gibson and Ibanez back in the '70s when Ibanez was making virtually exact replicas of classic Gibson designs, but when the lawyers went home, everyone shook hands and Ibanez has flourished by designing their own guitars. Today, the largest distributor of counterfeit guitars is by far China since it is very hard for American companies to get them to legally stop production. You can still find websites that feature some of the most sought after and highly-priced guitar examples from Gibson, Fender, Rickenbacker, Martin, and Paul Reed Smith. It is truly amazing how close they come to the originals (especially looking from a distance), but "God is in the details" and if you take your time and thoroughly look over a guitar you can determine its true origin.

As I was searching guitars on Craigslist, eBay, and every other reputable guitar dealer that I found in *Vintage Guitar* or *Premier Guitar,* I found a cheap Lucille. The problem was, it was too cheap and wasn't the Epiphone model. Upon closer inspection, I found that although the headstock looked close, the pickguard was totally wrong and the guitar input jack was on the top of the body! I pulled out books comparing other details like the placement of the Vari-Tone control and even the volume and tone controls, and everything was just slightly off. I also notified a few friends of mine at Gibson so they could follow up with the owner (who may have thought it was legit or a dealer who was trying to scam people). The problem with counterfeit guitars is when people who aren't extremely knowledgeable about a particular model or brand are duped into believing this is an authentic Gibson Lucille made in Memphis, Tennessee – when it isn't. What should be a two or three thousand dollar guitar is actually worth three or four hundred bucks, plus it won't sound or play as good as an original, and it can't be resold as an original!

Having owned a counterfeit Les Paul Custom myself, I can tell you the workmanship is sub-standard, wiring is cheap and not insulated, pickups are cheap and noisy, and the hardware is very low grade, especially the machine heads. If you are looking for a good quality Lucille, whether it is the Epiphone or the Gibson model, I recommend you buy from a reputable music store or a person you trust and check out everything from top to bottom before you lay down your hard-earned cash. Plenty of online research and a good value guide book like the *Blue Book of Electric/Acoustic Guitars* or *Gruhn's Guide to Vintage Guitars* can help you avoid many of the pitfalls that others have been trapped by! Knowledge is power, especially when dealing with vintage and used instruments, and as the counterfeiters are getting better at their reproductions, we as buyers must improve as well!

Chapter 35
LUCILLE HELD BY ANOTHER?

Although Lucille was built to B.B. King's exact specifications, a number of other top musicians have also been attracted to her style, tone, and playability. One of the most popular musicians, besides B.B., is Joe Perry from the band Aerosmith. But Perry's is named "Billie" after his wife and features a custom artist rendering of his spouse on the front of the body. From the Gibson guitar website, Perry stated, "First off, it's a B.B. King 'Lucille' guitar. We've made a few alterations, and of course it has a stunning picture of my wife on it. She's gorgeous, the guitar is gorgeous — how can I not look good playing it?" Perry can be seen at virtually every Aerosmith concert wielding this guitar and performing a number of their hit songs.

Many other musicians have also been known to play a Lucille on stage and in the studio. I spoke with Stacy Mitchhart, a local blues legend in Nashville and inductee to the 2012 South Canadian Blues Hall of Fame, and he told me the story of when a bar owner was so pleased with his music that he bought him a brand new Gibson Firebird guitar as a gift of thanks! The only problem was Stacy couldn't get his bluesy sound on stage with the Firebird, so he asked the owner if he would mind trading it back to the music store for the guitar of his dreams, a Gibson B.B. King Lucille in original Ebony finish! The owner was happy to abide by the request and the rest is blues history! Mitchhart is now endorsed by the Epiphone guitar division, a part of the Gibson brand family. 👑

Stacy Mitchhart is a local blues legend in Nashville and has recently become an endorser of Epiphone guitars. Shown with an Epiphone Sheraton II, Mitchhart attributes much of his bluesy sound to a Gibson B.B. King Lucille. Image courtesy Gibson Guitar Brands

Chapter 36
LUCILLE AMPLIFIED – B.B. KING'S AMPLIFIERS

Guitar amplifiers are frequently treated like stepchildren compared to their sexier and more attention-grabbing sibling, the guitar, but without a good amplifier no one can hear how truly great an electric guitar sounds! As any studio or stage guitarist will tell you, a good amplifier can definitely shape and make your tone!

As can be seen in pictures from the 1930s through today, B.B. King has used a variety of amplifiers to project the blues serenade of Lucille to his ever-faithful followers. In the early days, he followed the trends of the times utilizing vintage Fenders and Gibsons since those were virtually all that was available for guitar amplification in the 1930s, '40s, and '50s. When he was interviewed by Dan Erlewine, King stated, "And my first amplifier, the very first one I ever had, was a little Gibson amplifier with something like an 8" or 10" speaker in it – one speaker." Later on, he settled on one of Fender's bench mark amplifiers, the pre-CBS Fender Twin, for its consistent tone and the simplicity of setting knobs and adjustments. King kept using the older Fender Twin models, even after the newer Twins were launched with more wattage and increased tone shaping capabilities, but he preferred the simpler setup of the vintage amps. All of that changed when B.B. was approached by a friend of his that was now at Gibson – Dennis Chandler, and he brought with him their new line of Lab Series amps. Gibson, although their older tube amps are now becoming increasingly collectable, had never been a true player in the amplifier realm compared to Fender, Silvertone, and even Oahu in the early days. Although many of Gibson's tube amps through the '50s and '60s sound incredible, they just weren't as highly sought after by the public as Fender and Marshall amplifiers.

During the mid-1970s, Huck Daniels related, "B.B. used the SG (Systems) amps when we were recording back then and he got them for free from Gibson. He would use two of the big SG amps at once with the two twelves in them." SG System amplifiers were built by Chicago Musical Instrument Company (CMI) and were offered in popular amp and PA configurations that Gibson (Norlin) had a relationship with.

This series of amps may have harkened King's gradual move away from tube amplifiers since the SG System amps were hybrids, more like Music Man amplifiers (Leo Fender's next instrument line after leaving the Fender Musical Instrument Company and prior to G&L). They featured a solid-state preamp with tubes in the final power section. Wally Marx (author of *Gibson Amplifiers 1933-2008*) said, "The 8417 power tubes they used in the SG were very unique since they were some of the last newly designed power tubes to enter the market – and those tubes are hard to find now." My understanding is that the 8417 tubes stopped being manufactured in the late '80s, and to change over to a different type of power tube like 6L6 or EL34s requires other modifications to the SG amp. Besides the progressive tubes they used, the amps were known to be quite heavy and well-built since they were constructed like road cases. They are seldom seen in public today, but rumor has

Fender Twin Reverb
Courtesy Dave Rogers - Dave's Guitar Shop

Robert Garland (B.B. King's guitar and amp tech) and the author. Photography by Ted Vandell

Robert Garland leans back on one of King's Lab Series L5 amps to show the Peavey speakers. Photography by Ted Vandell

it that a few studios around the country still maintain an SG Series amp as a secret tone weapon in their arsenal. King moved from his favored Fender Twins to the SG amps as the Twins gained more knobs and effects that he didn't care for. The SG amps are easily identified by their larger '70s style knobs and retro looking amp chassis.

From my interview, Dennis Chandler stated, "In 1978, Lab Amps were launched and the first literature came out on them in 1977." He said that the pinnacle years for the Lab Amps were 1978, 1979, and 1980. The Norlin Company, who owned Gibson, also purchased Moog which was a forward-thinking synthesizer company at the time. The Moog team was asked to come up with a full line of solid-state amplifiers and they did just that, launching the amps from the Lincolnville, Illinois factory. None of the Lab Series amps bore the Gibson name, but they were obviously sold through Gibson's extensive distribution of dealers. Many popular musicians, besides B.B. King, such as Ronnie Montrose, Jim Messina, and even Les Paul were associated with the Lab brand of amps through advertising in popular guitar magazines. The Lab Series experiment only lasted through 1985, when the amp line was discontinued. Lab produced a full spread of amps, most featuring 100 solid-state watts; these included the L2 (head-only version), L3 (1x12 in. 60 watts), L4 (Bass amp 200 watts), L5 (2x12 in. 100 watts), L7 (4x10 in. 100 watts), and the L9 (1x15 in. 100 watts). The Lab Series 2 went on to add a few more amps during the early '80s, but the most successful of all of these amps was the L5, and long after the demise of the line, it continues to be the most sought out solid-state amp from this period.

Dennis Chandler stated, "I showed him [B.B. King] how to setup the amp. The setting you see in the print ad [ads featuring King and the amps] is how the amp is setup for B.B. to this day." The Lab Series L5 amps, which became B.B. King's favorite, are called a poor man's Fender Twin since they share many similarities like the 2 x 12 in. speaker construction and 100 watts of power. The major difference being the lack of preamp and power tubes the Fender amps utilize.

Here are the specifications for the L5 amp:

100 watts RMS into 8 ohms
Two 12 in. 16 ohm speakers
Two channels
Two inputs (high gain, low gain) per channel
Compressor
Reverb
Bright switch
Effects loop
Line out
Footswitch connector
Features

Front Panel Controls:

First channel
Bright switch
Volume
Bass, midrange, treble
Second channel
Bright switch
Volume
Bass (frequency, midrange), treble
Multifilter
Reverb
Compressor
On/off switch
Master volume
Power and compressor LEDs

Rear Panel Features:

Power amp input
Speaker output
Reverb on/off
Pre-amp output

Peavey Black Widow speaker as retrofitted in B.B. King's Lab Series L5 Amps. Courtesy Peavey Electronics Corporation

As verified by Dennis Chandler and B.B.'s amp tech, Robert Garland, King takes out the stock CTS speakers from every Lab Series amp he owns and has them replaced with Peavey Black Widow 12 in. speakers so he can increase the low end tones and the Peaveys handle higher wattage better. Chandler said, "B.B. went to the Peavey Black Widows in the early '80s."

Unfortunately with King's playing style on tour (usually the amps were turned up as loud as they would go) the DTS speakers would only last for two months with him. Of the Black Widow speaker models available, Garland told me that B.B. prefers model 1201-8.

Here are the stats for this particular speaker, from the Peavey website:

12"
Impedance: 8 Ohms
Power capacity: 1400 W Peak 700 W Program 350 W Continuous
Sensitivity: 98.5 dB / 1 W 1 m
Usable freq. range: 60 Hz ~ 3.5 kHz
Cone: Kevlar® impregnated cellulose
Voice coil diameter: 4.0" / 100 mm
Voice coil material: Aluminum ribbon wire Polyimide-impregnated fiberglass former Nomex® stiffener Solderless diffusion welded OFHC copper leads
Net weight lb. / kg: 16 lbs. / 7.3 kg
Znom (ohms) 8
Revc (ohms) 6.52
Sd (Square Meters) 0.052
BL (T/M) 19.60
Fo (Hz) 57.4
Vas (liters) 66.3
Cms (uM/N) 172.8
Mms (gm) 44.4
Qms 4.843
Qes 0.27
Qts 0.257
Xmax (mm) 2.60
Le (mH) 0.37
SPL (1W 1m) 98.5
No (%) 4.49%
Vd (cu. in. / ml) 16.5 / 270
Pmax (Watts pgm.) 700
Disp (cu. in. / ml) 109 / 1797
(source www.peavey.com)

Black Widow speaker marked for B.B. King at Robert Garland's workshop. Photography by Ted Vandell

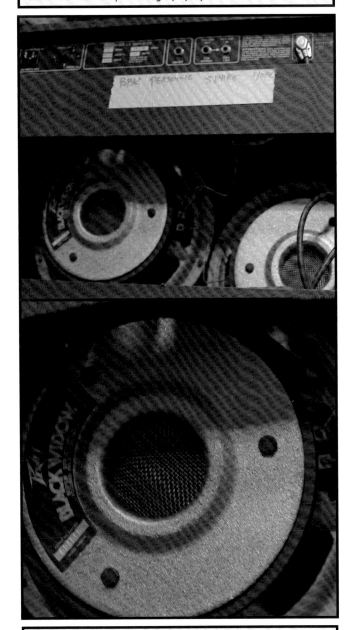

Back of Lab Series L5 with Black Widow speakers installed. Photography by Ted Vandell

The down side of converting to the Black Widow speakers is that they also add 20 more pounds to the overall weight of the amp due to the larger Peavey magnets. King has continued playing the Lab Series 5 amplifiers to this day, although he wears one out every few years and must have them restored or find another clean example. Huck Daniels said, "B.B. has those Lab amps all over his house." Dennis Chandler has also been in charge of tracking down replacement Lab amps for King and different guitars he has wanted to add to his collection as well. But King's fans also send him free Lab amps as an homage to his music, including Eric Johnson, who donated a Lab amp to B.B.'s amp stable featuring a brass plaque thanking King. When B.B. is touring in other countries, if he doesn't take one or two of his Labs, he typically requests a Fender Twin since that is as close as he can come to his beloved Lab amp on the road. But when he is touring in the States, he always provides his own Lab Series 5 to get his exact tone!

I had the good fortune to meet Hartley Peavey (Founder & CEO Peavey Electronics Corp) in person at a recent Winter NAMM show and he brought up how he and B.B. are friends. We then discussed my experience with Mr. King, and I brought up how he had been changing out the stock speakers in his Lab Series amps since the '80s with Peavey speakers. Hartley stated, "I never knew that. I'll have to bring that up next time I see him!" Mr. Peavey was an incredible interview (a legend in the music industry) and a very interesting man to speak with. Mr. Peavey was also kind enough to supply me with a picture for this publication of the Peavey Black Widow speaker that B.B. uses in all of his amps.

When his amps need repair, which is frequent after tours and due to the age of these discontinued amps, King depends on Robert Garland, who is the best kept amp secret in Las Vegas, and he's based out of the Sam Ash Music Store! Garland moved to Las Vegas in 1987, but now resides in Kingman, Arizona, with his family. He was also a luthier with Taylor guitars from 1997 to 1998, and even owned his own music store in Kingman. Since 2001, Garland has been a guitar and amp tech from what was Mars Music, which became Sam Ash at the same location. He commutes to work three days a week to the Las Vegas store and works on his own boutique amps, "Hillbilly Amplifiers," when he's at home and still plays the occasional rockabilly gig when he has time. Hillbilly Amplifiers was launched in 2006, and Garland custom builds each one to the customer's specifications, from the capacitors to tubes and of course the desired wattage!

From my interview, Garland told me that King currently has 30 Lab Series L5 amplifiers, and that he maintains five or six amps just to cannibalize parts from. Extra reverb tanks, which are common Accutronics and Beltron units, are kept at Garland's home for safe keeping. The spare Black Widow speakers are kept at the shop as are some of the extra Moog, Motorola, and Texas Instruments parts, which were popular in the late '70s. Even burnt up parts arc saved, as any piece of them may be salvaged and used to repair the next problem. As usual after a tour, King's and Charlie Dennis' Lab amps are both brought into Garland for repair; this time they were actually "dropped off of the back of a truck in their padded tour cases." As in the past, the amps were rolled into Garland's repair area in Sam Ash after they got off the road and were there waiting for him when he arrived for healing! More recently the King band came off of tour and the road manager, one of King's children, came in to talk with Garland and asked, "Didn't you fix these amps before we went out on the last tour?" This was in reference to the "Falling off the truck" incident. Of course Garland had thoroughly gone through and repaired both amplifiers so they were road ready. When they were brought back in this time, he found a sticker inside the amplifier sections and a letter from the TSA (Transportation Security Administration). Apparently, while the band was traveling through New York, the amps were disassembled, reviewed, approved (with stickers and a letter), and then not fully re-assembled. So for the entire tour, the Lab amps weren't functioning properly due to a security search. Garland was told by the road manager that they are looking into methods of shipping the amps and other important gear direct to the venues to avoid this in the future.

I also asked Garland about what kind of interesting items he found in the back opening of B.B.'s amps. It is a common habit for musicians to throw anything that is loose or sitting on top of the amp during a show into the back next to the speakers for storage and ease of moving. Garland told me how he had found guitar straps, cables, and the standard stuff you would expect to find in the back of any musician's

amp, but then I asked him what is the funniest thing you ever found in the back of B.B.'s amps? Garland said, "I find a lot of napkins with lipstick and phone numbers on them, and as far as I know, B.B. doesn't wear lipstick!" I personally think that it is pretty darn impressive for a musician in his 80s to still be wooing the ladies enough to get a napkin kiss and a number to call later after the gig! B.B. King is currently considering changing amplifiers (as clean examples of his favored Lab Amps become harder to find), and Robert Garland is working on a few Hillbilly Amplifier prototypes for King to test out on the road. On the most recent tours, King continues to use slightly modified, favored vintage L5 Lab Series amps for that pure B.B. tone! ♛

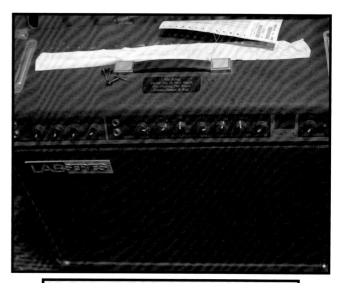

Lab Series L5 amp donated by blues fans.
Photography by Ted Vandell

Chapter 37
B.B.'S GUITAR CABLES

Every guitarist that is in pursuit of the ultimate tone knows that it doesn't take just a great guitar and amp, but also the conduit that transfers the sound waves from the guitar to the amp – guitar cables. B.B.'s amp/guitar technician, Robert Garland, said that he has seen a variety of guitar cables left in the back of his boss' amps. These cables have ranged from Ernie Ball, DiMarzio, Monster, and even George L's guitar cables. Charlie Dennis mentioned that both he and Mr. King both switched to $150 a piece guitar cables, but it took me a while to find out who manufactured these high end cables.

When I got the chance to interview Dennis again, after another touring leg that took him through Monaco and Rome with King's band, he stated the cables are Mogami Platinum guitar cables, "the ones with the red tips on the ends," and that they buy them from Guitar Center here in Las Vegas. King doesn't get involved in the purchase of the cables (it is handled

by the road manager) and Dennis said, "They are very thick cables!" The Mogami Platinum electric guitar cables are offered in lengths of 12, 20, 30, and 40 foot lengths. They also feature Neutrik Silent plugs, ultra high density 100% coverage copper spiral shielding, low loss cellular polyethylene insulation, conductive pvc, oxygen-free copper core, and a lifetime warranty.

Dennis also confirmed that the high end cables do make a big difference compared to others they have used in the past, and that they always place the red end of the cable into the guitar and the black plastic end goes into the amplifier. I have personally tried every guitar cable from RadioShack to the most expensive boutique guitar cables made, and you really can tell a difference, especially in the amount of bass frequency that is lost on a longer cable run. This is obviously proven with King's sound, as the better the cable relays the tone, the better the sound is translated to the amplifier for the end result – pure blues! 👑

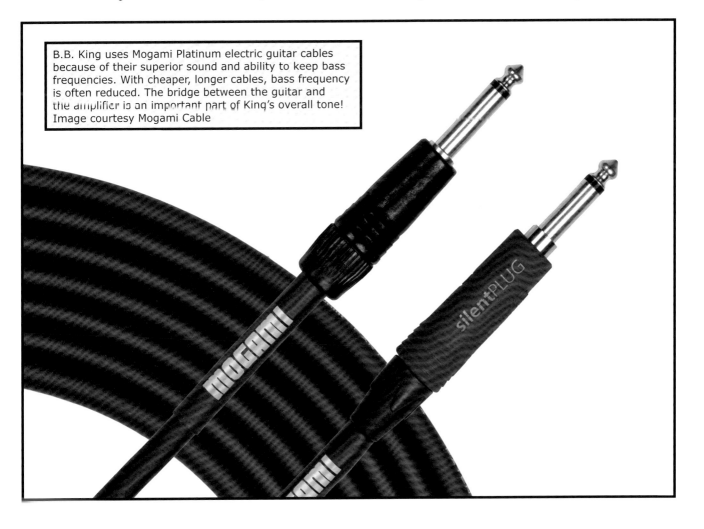

B.B. King uses Mogami Platinum electric guitar cables because of their superior sound and ability to keep bass frequencies. With cheaper, longer cables, bass frequency is often reduced. The bridge between the guitar and the amplifier is an important part of King's overall tone! Image courtesy Mogami Cable

Chapter 38
KING'S EFFECTS PEDAL – GUITAR PEDALS

Over the years, B.B. has used only one guitar effect that has been noted, preferring the natural sound of Lucille through a clean amplifier and just adjusting the tone and volume controls on the guitar for effect. In 1975, since it was all the rage at the time, he decided to try something new. The album was *Lucille Talks Back,* and it featured several tracks that used the extremely popular wah-wah pedal. King is quoted as saying that he used the wah pedal to try and give Lucille even more of a vocal quality on the album, which he has always been trying to achieve.

In September of 2010, I had a chance meeting with Huck Daniels, a local Las Vegas blues musician, at my local Guitar Center. While interviewing Huck, I asked what albums he had played on with King and the first one he rattled off was, *Lucille Talks Back.* Well as it ends up, Huck told me, "I gave B.B. the wah-wah pedal for that album since I had two of them,

and he was looking for a different sound." Since it was the mid-1970s Huck said, "No musician at that time could hit the stage without a wah pedal. I had three of them: two of the Original Thomas Organ Cry Babys and a Vox wah pedal that had fuzz on it, too. Those things went through batteries like crazy so I would keep one in the box so I could just change out the pedal since we were playing six hours a day." The wah-wah pedal that Daniels supposedly gave to King was the Original Cry Baby by Thomas Organ since he said it was the better pedal and not so wild sounding like the Vox. In fact, both the Cry Baby and Vox wah-wah pedals were made by VOX out of Italy, but Thomas Organ was the U.S. distributor and wanted their own pedal to market in the States. Therefore, VOX put the Cry Baby name on the front, since people compared the sound to that of a crying baby, and the rest is music history. Many other companies have emulated these original wah-wah pedals including Dunlop, Ibanez, Ernie Ball, Morley,

and numerous boutique pedal makers.

Fortunately, or unfortunately if you are a pedal manufacturer, King never used another guitar effects pedal for any recordings or live performances. Charles Dennis stated, "I haven't seen B.B. use any kind of effects pedal since I started touring with him back in 2001." Jason Toney, administrative assistant at the B.B. King Road Show office, recently had the good fortune to accompany Mr. King to the studio for a recording session in Las Vegas. One of the engineers in the studio was trying to get B.B. to use a wah-wah pedal in the session and King said, "I didn't like the way it [wah wah pedal] sounds, like it's auto tune for a singer. It seemed like the guitar was playing itself." From these comments, I believe it is safe to say that Mr. King won't be using any effects pedals again in the future, although he did for one album back in 1975! When King was asked by LaVerne Toney if Daniels was the person that provided him the wah-wah pedal for the original session, he stated, "Absolutely not!" But B.B. could also not offer the name of the person who did provide the pedal or if he bought it himself since it was so many years ago. King has also been quoted as saying, "I don't remember that kind of stuff, and I never was a technical person. Even when I knew I probably didn't know that one!" Mr. King may not know the details of specific guitars, pedals, amps, or even guitar cables, but all anyone really cares about is the end result – which is the music he continues to create with them! 👑

1970s Thomas Organ Cry Baby wah-wah pedal. Photography by Marc Kordalski

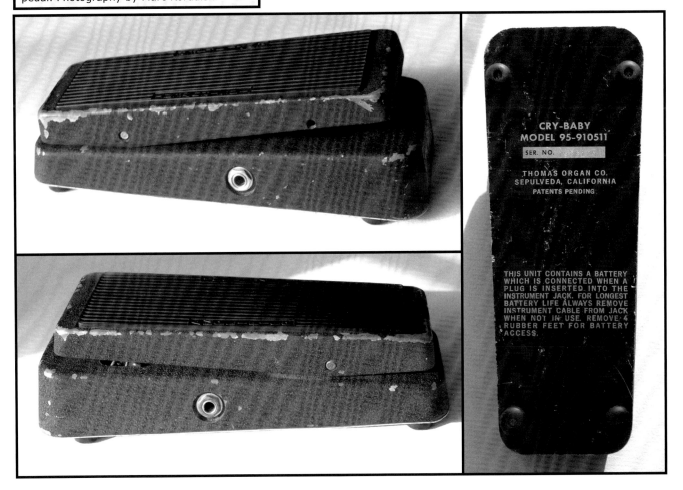

Chapter 39
PLECTRUMS OF A KING – GUITAR PICKS

Only the right kind of guitar pick can be used to strum and pick a guitar of Lucille's pedigree! Some players use their fingers, others use pesos, some guitarists use more obscure picks like wood, stone, ivory, and even vintage tortoiseshell – but not King. Charlie Dennis, his rhythm guitarist, uses Dunlop thumb picks and his fingers as frequently as he can. I'm not certain how many stories I have read and been told about B.B.King stopping into a local music store, in the town he would be playing a concert in that night, and buying some guitar picks. The question is, did he actually need picks or did he just want the camaraderie of stopping into a local music store and spending a little quality time with fellow musicians?

Whatever the case may be, in the early days, he would use a simulated tortoiseshell medium to thick gauge guitar pick, which was the standard at that time. Dennis Chandler said that with B.B., "Picks are all heavy!" As his popularity increased, especially after the chart-topping "The Thrill is Gone," he began using custom imprinted guitar picks made specifically for him. Examples of these picks vary with some featuring his signature, the country he was touring (i.e. Russia), the year of a tour, different pictures or poses of B.B. King, King and Lucille, and even his official website. Picks are also offered from all of his B.B. King Clubs as mementos from the visit to the establishment in that city. Some of the more obscure picks (and vintage ones from the '70s and '80s) have also become highly collectable, as can be seen on eBay and other guitar pick collecting websites. But being the gracious entertainer that he is, B.B. has always been known for handing these tools of the trade out to his fans at the end of his concerts as a way of thanking them for being such a great audience! After the final encore note is plucked on Lucille, one of his personal assistants helps King hand out his guitar picks to fans and he mixes in B.B. King necklaces, key chains, and even Lucille-shaped guitar pins as parting gifts to the crowd. ♛

Various B.B. King guitar picks from tours. Photography courtesy of Ted Vandell

Chapter 40
LUCILLE WITH STRINGS ATTACHED – GUITAR STRINGS

In the '60s, King was known for playing Fender Rock and Roll strings since they provided him an unwound G string. He has also been quoted as using Black Diamond guitar strings in his early days (verified by Dennis Chandler). But in the early '70s, the string of choice for B.B. became Gibson, although he has used Ernie Ball light top/heavy bottom strings briefly as well. In the 1980s, Gibson began producing B.B. King Signature strings in the gauge he prefers .54 (large E string) through .10 (small E string), which is considered a heavy top and light bottom.

The front cover has King's picture on the front and his signature appears just below the picture of the Lucille he is playing. I have personally found three different package cover pictures that have been used from the '80s through today. On the package it states that the strings are "Pure Nickel Wound Electric Guitar – B.B. King Signature Gauge." On the Gibson website, the strings are listed under accessories and the legendary strings section, which includes artist strings for Ace Frehley, B.B. King, Bill Monroe, Dickey Betts, Earl Scruggs, Les Paul, and Sam Bush. The website states the following, "B. B. plays with a style that matches his intensity, and every note he plays has something vitally important to say. This unique string set is B.B.'s own special gauge, meant to give your guitar a firm, yet extremely playable feel. The pure nickel wrap yields exceptional tone, from the lows all the way to the highs. The premium Swedish steel "hex" core means your guitar tunes up fast and stays in tune longer." Chandler stated that in the past, King has gone between 11s and 12s on the high E side of his guitar, and that in the old days, he changed strings all the time since they "would only sound good for six to eight hours." In the early days, B.B. would change all of the strings himself, and when he broke a string playing, it was usually the high E or B string, like most players, when he was bending strings during a solo. I have also heard stories of people seeing King in concert when he would break a string, never stop playing or singing, and would put on the new string on his guitar at the same time – that is talent under pressure!

Currently on the road, Charlie Dennis continues to restring B.B.'s Lucille with his Gibson signature strings;

B.B. King shown wailing away with Gibson guitar strings, circa 1970s.

although Gibson was going to stop manufacturing these in 2009, it appears they continue to make the King's strings. Charlie Dennis believes that even if Gibson stops manufacturing the strings for the public, they may continue creating the B.B. King Signature strings just for King to use on the road. Dennis, featuring more of a jazz approach to his blues playing style, special orders Thomastik-Infeld George Benson

Jazz Series GB114 from the Sam Ash store. These strings are gauged .014 to .055 and aren't carried in most music stores, plus he keeps them set at 440 standard tuning!

I asked Robert Garland about his days of working on King's guitars in Las Vegas when he would come off tour. Garland was always surprised that he over wound the strings around the tuning posts of his guitars when they came off the road, and he was instructed to do the same. Apparently in the 1930s and '40s, it was believed by many blues artists that winding the entire string around the tuning post added to the mass of the headstock with the metal and increased sustain. The truth of the matter is that this method actually adds to tuning problems as the string wire tries to settle into position between the other windings. King was already having tuning issues with some of his Lucilles that he took out on the road. So, Garland spoke to King's road manager at the time and asked him to speak to B.B. about cutting off the strings instead of winding them around the tuning post. After the road manager spoke to King, he called Garland back and said, "B.B. says he pays for the whole string, so he wants the whole string on there!" In the words of Garland, "How do you argue with that logic; it's B.B. King!"

What struck me as truly funny is that Dan Erlewine had a similar story about B.B. and the over winding of strings from back in 1992, and King stated that he and other blues players did this so they had extra string on the guitar in case one broke.

In 2002, B.B. continued to be plagued by tuning problems, so he bought all new Gold Gibson Stop Tailpieces and had Garland replace the tune-o-matic stop tailpieces with these on seven of his Lucilles. The problem was that as King rested his hand on the fine tuners of the tune-o-matic, it would make them move and go out of tune as he played. For several years, B.B. kept his main touring guitars in this configuration, and then he ended up switching most of them back to the original manufactured tune-o-matic fine tuner tail pieces. He seems to go back on forth on this issue depending on his tuning challenges at particular times; in the early '90s, he did the same thing. ♛

The stop tailpiece seen on this Lucille is one of the most common tailpieces used on non-vibrato/tremolo guitars. The stop tailpiece simply acts as a place for the strings to sit securely in at the bottom of the guitar. Image courtesy Eric Dahl/Marc Kordalski

Gibson Master Pack featuring B.B. King strings, strap, and picks. Photography by Ted Vandell

The fine-tune tailpiece on this Gem Lucille is considerably more complex than the stop tailpiece. Each string has an individual tuner that allows the player to make minor adjustments to the tuning without moving the tuning machines on the headstock. King tried the fine-tune tailpieces to help his tuning problems, but he rested his hand on the tailpiece when he played, therefore moving the tuners and putting the guitar out of tune. Image courtesy Eric Dahl/Marc Kordalski

Chapter 41
GUITAR STRAPS FOR LUCILLE

B.B. has been pictured using a wide variety of guitar straps to secure Lucille over his shoulder while playing concerts, many of which have been gifts from friends and fans. These have ranged from vintage thin leather straps, which were the standard in the 1930s through the 1950s, to custom made painted and hand tooled leather straps. The strap that accompanied the pawn shop 80th Birthday Lucille was a three inch wide Peavey that had very breathable material and of course the standard Schaller strap locks that King always uses. Robert Garland explained to me that as B.B. has gotten older, and had more challenges with his diabetes, he has taken to using straps that are better at keeping the sweat off of his shoulder – since a rash could cause serious problems with his illness. He has also become more selective on his straps since he is forced to sit while he plays most of the time, due to his back problems. Garland recalled, "B.B. brought in a custom red, white, and blue strap that he wanted strap locks on to use with Lucille. So I got everything set up, then the next thing I know I see him on TV using that exact strap a few days later."

Even though King primarily plays sitting down now he does still have his guitar tech install Schaller guitar strap locks on his straps and the Schaller buttons on the guitars he tours with. Schallers are made in Germany and come standard on many major manufactured guitars. ♔

B.B. King wearing one of his custom-made guitar straps.

Chapter 42
LUCILLE NUMBER 15 EXACT SPECIFICATIONS

In 1992, Dan Erlewine approached B.B. King about taking all of the measurements from his then current Lucille, number 15, as a bench mark to help blues players find what works best for them. Erlewine is a renowned luthier, author, musician, and repair method and tool innovator; he's also a great resource who constantly got back to me with answers! If you want to set up your guitar to be a B.B. King blues machine, here are the exact measurements Erlewine took from the Lucille King was playing on the road at that time.

Neck width: 1.698" at the nut, 2.055" at the 12th fret

Fret size: .098" wide x .045" (leveled and dressed the frets range from .038 to .045", with an average height of .040").

Pole piece height: Bridge position, 5/64" at the high E, 9/64" at the low E. Neck pickup's pole pieces are 9/64" at the high E, 13/64" at the low E.

Nut height/string clearance: (measured from the bottom of the string to the top of the 1st fret) .015" for the high E, .038" for the low. No open strings buzz.

Neck relief (measured at the 7th and 8th frets): .030", which is considered a high amount. .015" is considered normal.

String height at the 12th fret (bottom of outside E strings to the top of the 12th fret): All strings measured 7/64" in height across the board – a stiff and high action.

String Width at the nut (measured from the outside E to E): 1.425"

(Source *Guitar Player Repair Guide*, 1st Edition)

Courtesy *Guitar Player Repair Guide*, 1st Edition

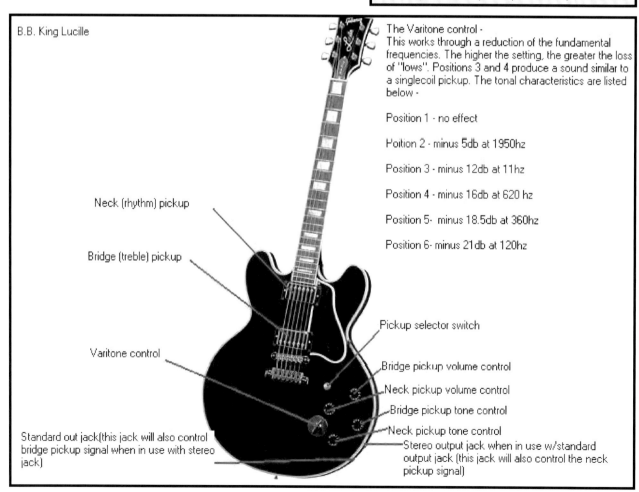

B.B. King Lucille

The Varitone control -
This works through a reduction of the fundamental frequencies. The higher the setting, the greater the loss of "lows". Positions 3 and 4 produce a sound similar to a singlecoil pickup. The tonal characteristics are listed below -

Position 1 - no effect

Poition 2 - minus 5db at 1950hz

Position 3 - minus 12db at 11hz

Position 4 - minus 16db at 620 hz

Position 5- minus 18.5db at 360hz

Position 6- minus 21db at 120hz

Neck (rhythm) pickup

Bridge (treble) pickup

Varitone control

Pickup selector switch

Bridge pickup volume control

Neck pickup volume control

Bridge pickup tone control

Neck pickup tone control

Standard out jack(this jack will also control bridge pickup signal when in use with stereo jack)

Stereo output jack when in use w/standard output jack (this jack will also control the neck pickup signal)

Chapter 43
LUCILLE – REPAIRS AND MAINTENANCE ON THE ROAD

King has been quoted as saying that early on he did his own repairs and restringing on the road, and when Lucille needed major repairs like fretwork or other issues, he would send them back to the Gibson factory! As B.B. edged his way into his 70s, he started relying on his rhythm guitarists to handle the duty of maintaining Lucille on the road. I had the pleasure of interviewing Charles (Charlie) Dennis, B.B. King's current rhythm guitarist in his band, and he filled in many facts for me, not to mention some great stories from the road.

Dennis was born in Shreveport, Louisiana, in 1948, and began playing guitar at the age of nine. By the time he was 11, Albert Collins' band would allow him on stage to play his guitar in the bars where they were booked. He has lived in Texas and California, before gravitating to Las Vegas, Nevada. He traveled the country with one of B.B.'s closest friend for two years during the 1980s – the late Bobby Bland, an awesome entertainer and blues singer in his own right. Dennis also had a band in California before moving to Las Vegas that included Keb' Mo' and Joe Albright. In 2000, while living in Las Vegas, Dennis formed his own popular band that played on the Strip called "Tune or Later," and he also backed up the band "Imperials" on rhythm and lead guitar

Dennis told me that over the years, B.B.'s rhythm guitarists have always assumed the duties of guitar tech maintaining his Lucilles on the road. Prior to 2002, King's rhythm guitarist, Leon Warren from January 15, 1982, through January 2, 2006, (when he passed away) carried out these same duties. Although Dennis had been on the Las Vegas music scene since 2000, he was ultimately found and recruited by King's long time keyboardist, James Toney. The story goes that Dennis was playing with his band at the Sand Dollar, a popular locals blues venue in Las Vegas and that night he covered one of B.B.'s songs, "Playin' with My Friends" while Toney was there. Usually Dennis didn't sing the B.B. songs he covered; he just backed up other singers, but for some reason this time he did and he sang it better than he ever had before. Toney ended up sitting in with the band and went back and told his boss about Dennis' playing. Dennis was hired to fill in with King's band while his regular guitarist, Leon Warren, recovered from medical issues.

Warren returned for a while, and Dennis continued as fill in at B.B.'s urging until Leon Warren passed away, at which point Charlie became a full-fledged member of Mr. King's band and has remained ever since. Dennis' main guitar of choice is a 2001 Gibson Byrdland that was gifted to him from B. B. King.

Charlie Dennis shown holding the Gibson Byrdland guitar that B.B. King gave him as a gift! Photography by Ted Vandell

Full shot - Charlie Dennis Gibson Byrdland guitar. Photography by Ted Vandell

After becoming the main guitarist with B.B., Dennis felt he needed to, "Get with the program and play a Gibson like the boss," instead of the Epiphone or George Benson guitars he usually played. So he talked with the Gibson representative about getting a Gibson Super 400, and they said he could have it at cost for $5,000 but he didn't have that kind of money.

So eventually the entire band was down in Memphis, and they stopped by the Gibson Custom Shop where B.B. told Dennis to play whatever he wanted and let him know what he liked. Dennis stated, "I go up to this guitar that is all surrounded by ropes and poles and I tell the Gibson people I wanna play that one. It ends up being a Custom Shop Gibson Byrdland that sold for twenty thousand bucks." He tried out several other Gibson guitars there, but nothing else felt or sounded the same, so he told B.B. which one he liked, but also that he didn't want King to think he was trying to take advantage of him. Dennis left the Gibson factory and headed back to the hotel to relax before the show that evening. Later that night, Dennis went to his dressing room to get ready for the show and there standing in the room was a Gibson representative guarding the Gibson Byrdland that Dennis had played earlier that day. The representative told him, "I sure am glad you finally got here so you can take your guitar; I was afraid to leave it."

Dennis has played that same guitar on every gig with B.B. King since that day. Along the way, he added to the pickguard two heart shaped earrings, which were a gift from Tina France, their tour manager while in New York City, and a Gibson pin from the Gibson Custom Shop. Besides changing out the metal tune-o-matic bridge to a wooden one, B.B. King's autograph on the upper bout, and Dunlop strap locks, it is all original. Dennis said the reason he changed out the bridge is, "I like the warmer sound of a wood bridge. That metallic sound of the tune-o-matic may work for some folks, but not me!" At one point, someone broke into Dennis' house in Las Vegas while he was on the road, and stole all of his other prized guitars except for the Gibson Byrdland he had out on tour with him. He doesn't take any back-up guitars on the road with him, but he does currently own a Martin D18, Epiphone Emperor Regent, and a new Ibanez

Montage Hybrid Cutaway acoustic electric guitar.

Besides his extremely important role as King's rhythm guitarist, his secondary job, as mentioned earlier, is the care and feeding of B.B.'s Lucilles while they are on the road. As Dennis explained to me," About three times a week, they bring one of B.B.'s Lucilles to my room and I restring her, tune her, and make sure she handles right and is clean." This is also usually accompanied with an envelope that contains some money in it as a way to thank Dennis for the extra work he is providing. Dennis has put together his own guitar tech tool box, which includes a Boss tuner, Fender foot pedal tuner, wire cutters, and other adjustment necessities. On a typical tour, B.B. takes two Lucilles so he has one as a back-up in case something major goes wrong, etc., but he usually plays the same one all of the time. Dennis explained that he personally does all of the minor maintenance on the road including adjusting the truss rod in the neck (to maintain the correct relief) and adjusting string height, etc., but when it comes to electronics or other major problems, it goes back to Robert Garland in Las Vegas (like the amplifiers).

In the summer of 2010, B.B. and his band came off tour and Charlie Dennis stopped by the Sam Ash Music Store to talk with Garland. Apparently on this last leg of the tour, King wasn't happy with how Dennis was stringing up Lucille and he wanted the strings "locked" (a term that means the end of the string that is around the tuner is cut off and bent around itself to better secure the string and avoid slippage) like Garland had been doing for him. To encourage Dennis to learn how to do this, B.B. had cut Dennis' guitar set up fee in half until he did it right! Dennis got Garland to show him how he was winding the strings and will take these skills back on the road so he can return to full set up for the August gigs! Dennis is happy to oblige to whatever detailed requests King may want handled on the road as he stated, "B.B. is the best bandleader I have ever played for, and he takes good care of his band." ♔

Closeup of pickguard - Charlie Dennis Gibson Byrdland guitar. Photography by Ted Vandell

Chapter 44
LUCILLE NUMBER 18 AND COUNTING!

Since the original naming of B.B. King's guitar on that fateful morning in Twist, Arkansas, back in 1949, there has been a total of 18 Lucilles to date. Only the guitars that actually go out on tour and are played at the shows are given a Lucille number designation. His assistant LaVerne Toney told me that he vaults the ones he doesn't use anymore to save them. She also told me that he has never given away any of his personal Lucilles to any friends or family members, except for one that he gave to a grandchild and the 80th Birthday Prototype #2 that he gave to his son Willie. It would seem logical that all of his remaining guitar and amp collection would remain as part of his estate and legacy for his children, grandchildren, great-grandchildren, and so on. Patty King, one of B.B.'s daughters, told me that four guitars from his Lucille collection are now being exhibited at the B.B. King and Delta Interpretive Center Museum in Indianola, Mississippi. She stated that several of the heads of the museum came to Las Vegas and were allowed to go through his collection and pick the pieces that were most suitable for display there.

It's hard to say how many more Lucilles will grace the stage with Mr. King. At 87 years young, he appears to have no inclination to slow down his schedule of tours. When I caught up with him in between tour dates in 2009, he said, "I gotta get back on the road and earn some money." Although after all of these years and with wisely-placed investments it would seem unlikely that money is the true drive for Mr. King to get back out on the road. I believe that the road is actually the only true home he knows now, and everywhere else is just a stop over in between the next concert or the next recording session. I have been told recently that his personal assistant on the road, Myron Johnson, has now been placed in charge of the security, handling, and general overseeing of Mr. King's Prototype #1 80th Birthday Lucille, as that is the only one he continues to play on the road after its return. 👑

B.B. King looking down at his returned 80th Birthday Lucille. Photography by Ted Vandell

Chapter 45
TALES OF LUCILLE

As traveling companions since 1949, when the name Lucille was first applied to his beloved guitar, and in the 33 years she has been a Gibson B.B. King Lucille signature model, B.B. has traveled more miles and to more cities and countries with his guitars than any band member or loved one! This would obviously provide some unique stories and life experiences like the Twist, Arkansas story from back in 1949, where Lucille got her name. In one case, Lucille actually saved B.B. King's life when a car started to roll over on him but the case kept the car propped up so it didn't crush him.

In another instance, Lucille was left inside a local tavern (the Red Light Inn) after a weekend of gigging back in the late '40s in Covington, Kentucky. Vincent (Red) Doss told me (as I interviewed him at Guetterman Motors in Cairo, Illinois) that his route took him from Memphis up to Covington back in those days, and that B.B. was staying in a one-room apartment down in Memphis, but would play up in Covington all the time. He first met King as he was walking through a mud-filled road to get to his gig up in Covington, and Red gave him a ride when he was headed to the Cotton Club, another popular bar. This became a regular occurrence, and he would also drive him to the Red Light Inn since he was friends with Norris Nicks, the owner. At some point, a disagreement happened with the other Nicks brother and an angry competing bar owner put a case of dynamite at the front door on a Sunday night. Red said that B.B. and the rest of the band had left all of their gear in the club after gigging there on Friday and Saturday night. By the time King got there to assess the damage, he found his guitar blown all the way up into a tree!

King has also used Lucille as an Olive Branch, giving Lucille guitars to presidents, popes, fellow musicians, numerous charities, and even as a reward for his lost dog in 2006. Apparently B.B.'s canine companion (also named Lucille), a two-year-old white female Maltese, went missing while staying in West Hollywood under the care of his co-manager, Matthew Lieberman. After ten days had passed and over 500 signs had been put up trying to secure the return of Lucille, King decided to offer a signed Lucille guitar in return for his puppy! I never found a follow up article, but my bet is that the guitar as a reward did work! 👑

B.B. King telling stories at the November 30th, 2009 meeting at his Las Vegas office. Photography by Ted Vandell

Chapter 46
MAGIC

King has been married twice, without having children with either spouse, but he has fathered 15 children (that he acknowledges as his own) by 15 different women through his journeys. I have had the pleasure to meet and speak with several of the kids and though B.B. was an absentee father, he has tried to make it up to all of them in his own way by helping out financially when he can and by paying for all of his children's and grandchildren's college tuitions if they attend.

King's current lineup of band members includes: James Bolden – trumpet; Herman Jackson – drums/percussion; Melvin Jackson – saxophone; Stanley Abernathy – trumpet; Charles Dennis – guitar; Reggie Richards – bass guitar; Walter King – saxophone; and Ernest Vantrees – piano/keyboards. When you speak to anyone who has worked for or with B.B., or even his family members, there is a certain reverence and respect for the man that transcends his music and talents. Anyone who has ever met him, talked with him, watched him perform, or had the honor of performing with him on stage knows exactly what I'm speaking of. Charles Dennis, his rhythm guitarist since 2002, summed it up in one word: "Magic." Unless you use a more biblical reference, since B.B. and most of his family members are firm in their religious beliefs, then "Magic" is probably as fitting a term as any. Dennis related some stories to me that he said are just a few instances of what consistently happens on the road with King. Since they frequently travel overseas to tour they are forced to fly a lot, something that B.B. isn't too fond of since he prefers his personally decked out tour bus for ultimate comfort. Apparently it has been noted that anytime King is on the plane there is no turbulence and the flight is a cruise, but when he isn't on the plane with the band then it is a bumpy traveling experience. Similarly, when the band has played outdoor concerts and it has been storming and raining, somehow when B.B. takes the stage the bad weather stops. Then when he leaves the stage after the performance, the ill weather resumes its course.

Stories like these just add to the myth and mystery of a man who has out lived, out gigged, and out played almost all of his blues contemporaries, has continued to log 250 or more concerts per year at the age of 87, and is still going! Charlie Dennis also spoke at length about B.B.'s never-ending energy and that he has actually seen him working on a computer for over 15 hours straight! Dennis also has watched King sign over 200 autographs for his fans in one night after playing a full show! Dennis states the years haven't slowed B.B. down a bit and that his own fight with diabetes and other family problems have only added to his music, and it "comes out in his blues." King once told Dennis, "When I go, I want to be on a stage, on the way to a gig, or on top of a pretty woman!" Since he is the King of the Blues, I hope that B.B. King is granted one of his final wishes. In the spring of 2013, King had cut back his touring to just 100 gigs per year and he was still selling sold out concerts in Brazil and everywhere else he and his band traveled. ♔

A Swedish Gibson ad featuring B.B. King.

B.B. King in a Lab Series L5 amp advertisement.

Chapter 47
LUCILLE HAS LEFT THE BUILDING

I hope you have enjoyed reading this book as much as I have enjoyed researching it, conducting the one-on-one interviews, and writing it! I'm certain that some guitars and other details have fallen through the cracks, but my goal in writing this book was to gather as much information as possible about Mr. King's guitars and other gear while he and most of the behind the scenes people are still around to lend their voice and information to this tome. I have seen pictures where B.B. is holding every conceivable guitar known to man from a Gretsch electric to a National Resonator!

But the instruments mentioned within these pages, his Lab amps, and other accessories are the ones that he acknowledges using on a frequent basis. Besides a deeper knowledge of Mr. King's tools of the trade, I hope this book also motivates you to dig deeper into the musical well known as the blues and appreciate the talented men and women who brought us this incredible genre of music just for the joy of making it and sharing it. 👑

The information, specifications, and values contained in the following eight pages are taken from the *Blue Book of Electric Guitars* database. Specifications are compiled from a variety of sources including Gibson catalogs and spec sheets, Gibson books, and physical inspection/measurements of actual Gibson instruments. Values are computed based on actual selling prices commonly referred to as private party values (not retail or wholesale prices). Values are also determined based on the average selling price as this can vary between geographic regions and depending on economic conditions. For more information, please reference the *Blue Book of Electric Guitars* or visit www.bluebookofguitarvalues.com

B.B. KING STANDARD/LUCILLE STANDARD

Style: symmetrical double rounded cutaway ES-335-style semi-hollow body

Top: arched maple

Back/Sides: maple

F-holes: none

Binding: multi-ply top and back

Neck: set maple

Number of Frets: 22

Fretboard: bound rosewood with pearl dot inlays

Headstock: black overlay with pearl Gibson logo and Lucille inlays

Tuners: three-per-side

Bridge: tune-o-matic

Tailpiece: TP-6 tunable stop

Pickguard: raised layered black

Pickups: two covered humbuckers

Electronics: stereo

Knobs: four (two volume, two tone)

Pickup Switch: three-way

Output Jacks: two 1/4 in.

Hardware: chrome

Finishes: Cherry, Ebony

Years Manufactured: 1980-1985

Scale: 24.75 inches

Body Width: 16 inches

Body Depth: 2.25 inches

Blue Book values:

Grading	100% NEW	98% MINT	95% EXC+	90% EXC	80% VG+	70% VG	60% G
	N/A	$2,100	$1,675	$1,375	$1,050	$850	$675

Add 10% for Cherry finish.

This model was originally called the B.B. King Standard, and in 1981, it was renamed the Lucille Standard.

B.B. KING CUSTOM/LUCILLE CUSTOM/B.B. KING LUCILLE (MODEL ARLC)

Style: Symmetrical double rounded cutaway ES-335-style semi-hollow body

Top Wood: Arched maple top

Back/Side Wood: Maple back and sides

F-Holes: None

Binding: Multi-ply top and back

Neck: Set maple

Number of Frets: 22

Fretboard: Bound ebony with large pearl block inlays

Headstock: Multi-ply bound with black overlay and pearl Gibson logo and Lucille inlays (1980-circa 2007) or custom B.B. King inlay and graphics and a gold "Lucille" inscribed truss rod cover (circa 2007-present)

Tuners: Three-per-side

Bridge: Nashville tune-o-matic

Tailpiece: TP-6 tunable stop

Pickguard: Raised layered bound tortoise

Pickups: Two covered humbucker

Electronics: Stereo

Knobs: Four (two volume, two tone)

Pickup Switch: Three-way pickup

Other Switches: Vari-Tone rotary tone knob

Output Jack: Two 1/4 in. outputs

Hardware: Gold

Finishes: Cherry/Wine Red, Ebony, Beale Street Blue (2002-04)

Years Produced: 1980-present

Production Location: Kalamazoo (1980-1982), Nashville (1982-2001), Memphis (2001-present)

Gibson Model Code: ARLC

Scale: 24.75 inches

Body Width: 16 inches

Body Depth: 2.25 inches

Serial Numbers: Gibson's standard 8-digit serialization system with the exception of 1994 when all serial numbers start with "94"

Blue Book values:

Grading	100% NEW	98% MINT	95% EXC+	90% EXC	80% VG+	70% VG	60% G
1980-1989	N/A	$1,750	$1,400	$1,125	$875	$700	$575
1990-2001	N/A	$2,150	$1,725	$1,400	$1,075	$850	$700
2002-Present MSR $5,410	$3,800	$2,500	$2,000	$1,625	$1,350	$1,150	$1,000

Add 10% for Cherry/Wine Red finish.

This model was originally called the B.B. King Custom, in 1981 it was renamed the Lucille Custom, and in 1986, it was renamed the B.B. King Lucille. In circa 2007, the headstock was redesigned with a new B.B. King custom logo and graphics that did not feature the Gibson logo. This instrument was recently produced in the Gibson Memphis factory.

B.B. KING LUCILLE GEM SERIES

Style: Symmetrical double rounded cutaway ES-335-style semi-hollow body

Top Wood: Arched maple top

Back/Side Wood: Maple back and sides

F-Holes: None

Binding: Multi-ply top and back

Neck: Set maple

Number of Frets: 22

Fretboard: Bound ebony with large pearl block inlays

Headstock: Multi-ply bound with black overlay, custom B.B. King inlay, and graphics, and a gold "Lucille" inscribed truss rod cover

Tuners: Three-per-side

Bridge: Nashville tune-o-matic

Tailpiece: TP-6 tunable stop

Pickguard: Raised layered bound tortoise

Pickups: Two covered humbucker

Electronics: Stereo

Knobs: Four (two volume, two tone)

Pickup Switch: Three-way pickup

Other Switches: Vari-Tone rotary tone knob

Output Jack: Two 1/4 in. outputs

Hardware: Gold

Finishes: Amethyst (purple), Diamond (white), Emerald (green), Ruby (red), or Sapphire (blue)

Years Produced: Late 2010-2011

Production Location: Memphis

Gibson Model Code: N/A

Scale: 24.75 inches

Body Width: 16.25 inches

Body Depth: 2.25 inches

Unique Features: Limited production of 25 instruments in each finish (125 total created for the public although King was also given one of each color, bringing the total to 130), B.B. King Certificate of Authenticity booklet color matched to guitar with color and serial number inside, also included *The Best of B.B. King Christmas Collection* CD and *The B.B. King Treasures* hardbound book, launched through Musician's Friend's Private Reserve division

Serial Numbers: The B.B. King Lucille Gem Series was serial numbered "BBK0NNN." For example, the 120th guitar of the series has the serial number "BBK0120."

Blue Book values:

Grading	100% NEW	98% MINT	95% EXC+	90% EXC	80% VG+	70% VG	60% G
	$3,700	$3,050	$2,500	N/A	N/A	N/A	N/A

Last MSR was $5,175.

The B.B. King Lucille Gem Series was serial numbered "BBK0NNN." For example, the 120th guitar of the series has the serial number "BBK0120."

B.B. KING LUCILLE WITH B.B. KING SIGNATURE OR LUCILLE INLAYED FINGERBOARD

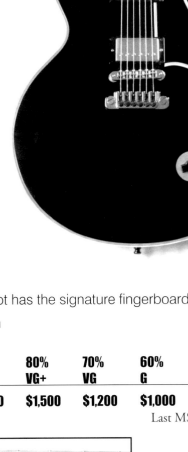

Style: Symmetrical double rounded cutaway ES-335-style semi-hollow body

Top Wood: Arched maple top

Back/Side Wood: Maple back and sides

F-Holes: None

Binding: Multi-ply top and back

Neck: Set maple

Number of Frets: 22

Fretboard: Bound ebony with "B.B. King" and two guitars inlaid in pearl

Headstock: Multi-ply bound with black overlay and pearl Gibson logo and Lucille inlays

Tuners: Three-per-side

Bridge: Nashville tune-o-matic

Tailpiece: TP-6 tunable stop

Pickguard: Raised layered bound black or tortoise

Pickups: Two covered humbucker

Electronics: Stereo

Knobs: Four (two volume, two tone)

Pickup Switch: Three-way pickup

Other Switches: Vari-Tone rotary tone knob

Output Jack: Two 1/4 in. outputs

Hardware: Gold

Finishes: Ebony

Years Produced: Mid-2002-2004

Production Location: Memphis

Gibson Model Code: ARBB

Scale: 24.75 inches

Body Width: 16 inches

Body Depth: 2.25 inches

Unique Features: Same as the B.B. King Custom Lucille, except has the signature fingerboard

Serial Numbers: Gibson's standard 8-digit serialization system

Blue Book values:

Grading	100% NEW	98% MINT	95% EXC+	90% EXC	80% VG+	70% VG	60% G
	N/A	$3,000	$2,400	$1,950	$1,500	$1,200	$1,000

Last MSR was $4,047.

B.B. KING SUPER LUCILLE

Style: Symmetrical double rounded cutaway ES-335-style semi-hollow body

Top Wood: Arched maple top

Back/Side Wood: Maple back and sides

F-Holes: None

Binding: Multi-ply top and back

Neck: Set maple

Number of Frets: 22

Fretboard: Bound ebony with abalone block inlays

Headstock: Multi-ply bound with black overlay, abalone Gibson logo, and Lucille inlays

Tuners: Three-per-side

Bridge: Nashville tune-o-matic

Tailpiece: TP-6 tunable stop

Pickguard: Hand-signed raised layered tortoise

Pickups: Two covered humbucker

Electronics: Stereo

Knobs: Four (two volume, two tone)

Pickup Switch: Three-way pickup

Other Switches: Vari-Tone rotary tone knob

Output Jack: Two 1/4 in. outputs

Hardware: Gold

Finishes: Black Sparkle

Years Produced: Mid-2002-2004

Production Location: Nashville – Custom Shop

Gibson Model Code: ARLS

Scale: 24.75 inches

Body Width: 16 inches

Body Depth: 2.25 inches

Unique Features: In 2004, Gibson produced 17 Super Lucilles as "Artist Proofs" to raise money for the Diabetes Foundation (B.B. King was given #18 for his involvement). These guitars have "Artist Proof" written in directly below the serial number, have a silver medallion below that (with NM, for Neiman Marcus, a star, and the number out of the 17 it is), and have a medallion on the front. The guitar body is hand signed instead of the pickguard on these Artist Proofs, or Neiman Marcus Lucilles as they are called. A leather-bound picture book of the signing with other details to send the guitar back to Gibson to clear coat the signature was included as well. The Custom Shop Certification individually numbers which one out of the 17 it is. These guitars were sold through Neiman Marcus and the number 17 represents the 17 million Americans living with diabetes, which B.B. King also suffers from, in 2004.

Serial Numbers: Super Lucille = Gibson's standard 8-digit serialization system Neiman Marcus = CS + 5 digits

Blue Book values:

Grading	100% NEW	98% MINT	95% EXC+	90% EXC	80% VG+	70% VG	60% G
	N/A	$3,500	$2,800	$2,250	$1,700	$1,300	$1,050

Last MSR was $4,000.

Add 20-25% for "Artist Proof" Neiman Marcus diabetes limited editions.

B.B. KING 80TH BIRTHDAY LUCILLE

Style: Symmetrical double rounded cutaway ES-335-style semi-hollow body

Top Wood: Arched maple top

Back/Side Wood: Maple back and sides

F-Holes: None

Binding: Multi-ply top and back

Neck: Set three-piece maple

Number of Frets: 22

Fretboard: Bound ebony with pearl block inlays

Headstock: Multi-ply bound with black overlay, B.B. King 80th Birthday inlays, and gold "Gibson" inscribed truss rod cover

Tuners: Three-per-side

Bridge: Nashville tune-o-matic

Tailpiece: TP-6 tunable stop

Pickguard: Raised engraved gold-bound black pickguard with B.B. King signature and crown logo

Pickups: Two covered B.B. King engraved humbucker

Electronics: Stereo

Knobs: Four gold UFO with mother-of-pearl inserts (two volume, two tone)

Pickup Switch: Three-way pickup

Other Switches: Vari-Tone rotary tone knob

Output Jack: Two 1/4 in. outputs

Hardware: Gold

Finishes: Black Pearl

Years Produced: 2006

Production Location: Nashville – Custom Shop

Gibson Model Code: N/A

Scale: 24.75 inches

Body Width: 16 inches

Body Depth: 2.25 inches

Unique Features: Black levant case and personally signed certificate of authenticity included, limited edition run of 82 instruments (80 guitars plus 2 prototypes). The headstock design and inlays match the artwork on B.B. King's 80 album, which is a birthday tribute to King.

Serial Numbers: Gibson's standard 8-digit serialization system + handwritten # of 80 under serial number

Blue Book values:

Grading	100% NEW	98% MINT	95% EXC+	90% EXC	80% VG+	70% VG	60% G
	N/A	$7,000	$5,600	$4,450	$3,500	$2,800	$2,275

Last MSR was $9,840.

B.B. KING "KING OF THE BLUES"

Style: Symmetrical double rounded cutaway ES-335-style semi-hollow body

Top Wood: Arched maple top

Back/Side Wood: Maple back and sides

F-Holes: None

Binding: Multi-ply top and back

Neck: Set three-piece maple

Number of Frets: 22

Fretboard: Bound ebony with pearl block inlays

Headstock: Multi-ply bound with black overlay and Gibson logo, gold truss rod cover, pearl plaque on the back reflecting the individual number out of 150

Tuners: Three-per-side

Bridge: Nashville tune-o-matic

Tailpiece: TP-6 tunable stop

Pickguard: Raised unbound pickguard with hand-drawn "Crown" and "King of Blues" inscription logos

Pickups: Two covered humbucker

Electronics: Stereo

Knobs: Four amber with silver inserts (two volume, two tone)

Pickup Switch: Three-way pickup

Other Switches: Vari-Tone rotary tone knob

Output Jack: Two 1/4 in. outputs

Hardware: Gold

Finishes: Ebony

Years Produced: 2006

Production Location: Nashville – Custom Shop

Gibson Model Code: N/A

Scale: 24.75 inches

Body Width: 16.1875 inches

Body Depth: 2.25 inches

Unique Features: Black levant case, limited edition run of 150 instruments. This guitar was built and sold exclusively for Guitar Center.

Serial Numbers: Gibson's standard 8-digit serialization system + plaque underneath with # of 150

Blue Book values:

Grading	100% NEW	98% MINT	95% EXC+	90% EXC	80% VG+	70% VG	60% G
	N/A	$4,000	$3,200	$2,600	$2,100	$1,700	$1,350

Last MSR was $4,700.

LITTLE LUCILLE

Style: Single sharp cutaway Blueshawk-style

Top Wood: Maple top

Back/Side Wood: Poplar

F-Holes: Two

Binding: Single-ply cream body

Neck: Set narrow mahogany with slight V shape

Number of Frets: 22

Fretboard: Bound rosewood with diamond inlays

Headstock: Black overlay with pearl Gibson logo, gold "B.B. King" engraved truss rod cover

Tuners: Three-per-side

Bridge: Nashville tune-o-matic

Tailpiece: TP-6 tunable stop

Pickguard: None

Pickups: Two Blues 90 with hum cancelling dummy coil

Electronics: Mono

Knobs: Two black numbered with gold inserts (volume, tone with push/pull Vari-tone disable)

Pickup Switch: Three-way pickup

Other Switches: Six-way Vari-Tone rotary tone knob

Output Jack: Two 1/4 in. outputs

Hardware: Gold

Finishes: Ebony, Blues Burst (2002-04), Wine Red (2002-04)

Years Produced: 1999-2004

Production Location: Nashville (1999-2002), Memphis (2002-2004)

Gibson Model Code: DSLL

Scale: 25.5 inches

Body Width: 13 inches

Body Depth: 1.75 inches

Unique Features: Painted "Little Lucille" on body next to start of the fingerboard.

Serial Numbers: Gibson's standard 8-digit serialization system

Blue Book values:

Grading	100% NEW	98% MINT	95% EXC+	90% EXC	80% VG+	70% VG	60% G
	N/A	$1,500	$1,200	$950	$775	$650	$525

Last MSR was $1,700.

Add 10% for Wine Red finish.

EPIPHONE B.B. KING LUCILLE

Style: Symmetrical double rounded cutaway ES-335-style semi-hollow body

Top Wood: Arched maple top

Back/Side Wood: Maple back and sides

F-Holes: None

Binding: Multi-ply top and back

Neck: Set maple

Number of Frets: 22

Fretboard: Bound rosewood with large pearl block inlays

Headstock: Multi-ply bound with black overlay and pearl Epiphone logo and Lucille script inlay

Tuners: Three-per-side

Bridge: Tune-o-matic

Tailpiece: Tunable stop

Pickguard: Raised layered bound tortoise with "E" logo

Pickups: Two covered humbucker

Electronics: Stereo

Knobs: Four black barrel (two volume, two tone)

Pickup Switch: Three-way pickup

Other Switches: Vari-Tone rotary tone knob

Output Jack: Two 1/4 in. outputs

Hardware: Gold

Finishes: Ebony

Years Produced: 1997-present

Production Location: Korea (1997-2004), China (2004-present)

Gibson Model Code: ETBB

Scale: 24.75 inches

Body Width: 16 inches

Body Depth: 1.875 inches

Serial Numbers: Epiphone's standard system of identifying the country of origin by a single letter followed by one or two digits indicating the last one or two digits of the year

Blue Book values:

Grading	100% NEW	98% MINT	95% EXC+	90% EXC	80% VG+	70% VG	60% G
MSR $1,165	$700	$550	$475	$400	$350	$300	$250

BIBLIOGRAPHY, WEBSITES, & INTERVIEWS

BIBLIOGRAPHY

Bacon, Tony. *Electric Guitars The Illustrated Encyclopedia.* San Diego, CA: Thunder Bay Press, 2000.

Batey, Rick. *The American Blues Guitar.* Milwaukee, WI: Hal Leonard Corporation, 2003

Carter, Walter. *Gibson Guitars: 100 Years of an American Icon.* Gibson Guitar Corp, 1994

Douse, Cliff. *100 Guitar Heroes.* United Kingdom: Future Publishing, Ltd., 2009

Duchossoir, A.R. *The Fender Telecaster.* Hal Leonard Corporation, 1991

Erlewine, Dan. *Guitar Player Repair Guide.* San Francisco, CA: Miller Freeman Books, 1994

Evans, Tom and Mary Anne. *Guitars from Renaissance to Rock* New York, NY: Facts on File, 1977

Fjestad, Zachary R. *Blue Book of Electric Guitars* (13th and 14th Editions). Minneapolis, MN: Blue Book Publications, 2011-13.

Freeth, Nick and Charles Alexander. *The Guitar.* Philadelphia, PA: Running Press Book Publishers, 2002

Freeth, Nick. *The Illustrated Directory of Guitars.* New York, NY: Barnes & Noble Books, 2004

Greenwood, Alan and Gil Hembree. *Vintage Guitar Price Guide 2010.* Bismarck, ND: Vintage Guitar Books, 2009

Gress, Jesse. *Original B.B. King.* New York, NY: Amsco Publications, 1989

Gruhn, George and Walter Carter. *Gruhn's Guide to Vintage Guitars.* San Francisco, CA: Miller Freeman Inc., 1991

Harpe, Neil. *Stella Guitar Book,* 2005

Ingram, Adrian. *The Gibson ES335 Story.* Anaheim Hills, CA: Centerstream Publishing LLC, 2006

King, B.B. and David Ritz. *Blues All Around Me.* New York, NY: Avon Books, 1996

Kostelanetz, Richard. *The B.B. King Companion – Five Decades of Commentary.* New York, NY: Schirmer Books, 1997

Marx, Jr., Wallace. *Gibson Amplifiers 1933-2008: 75 Years of the Gold Tone.* Minneapolis, MN: Blue Book Publications, Inc., 2009

McGee, David. *B.B. King There is Always One More Time.* San Francisco, CA: Backbeat Books, 2005

Moseley, Willie G. *Guitar People.* Bismarck, MD: Vintage Guitar Books, 1997

Obrecht, Jas. *Blues Guitar.* San Francisco, CA: Miller Freeman Books, 1993

Poe, Randy. *Squeeze My Lemon.* Milwaukee, WI: Hal Leonard Corporation, 2003

Russell, Tony. *The Blues.* New York, NY: Schirmer Books, 1992

Sawyer, Charles. *The Arrival of B.B. King.* Garden City, NY: Doubleday & Company, Inc., 1980

Schroeter, John August. *Between the Strings.* Colorado Springs, CO: John August Music, 2004

WEBSITES

Harmonycentral.com

Premier Guitar Magazine and www.premierguitar.com

Vintage Guitar Magazine and vintageguitar.com

Dennis Chandler : www.dennischandler.com

Gibson Corporation : www.gibson.com

B.B. King : www.bbking.com

http://www.vintageguitars.org.uk/gibsonES355TDSV_2.php

Peavey Electronics Official : www.peavey.com

INTERVIEWS

Bruce J. Kunkel – Master Luthier/ Creator of Art Guitars at the Gibson Custom Shop

Mike McGuire – Past Gibson Custom Shop Manager

Anthony Braggs – Past Gibson Custom Shop Staff

Dumitru (Dino) Muradian – Artist/Pyrographer

Tony Coleman – Percussionist/Drummer formerly with B.B. King

Dennis (D.C.) Chandler – Past Gibson Employee – Lucille's Godfather

Charles (Charlie) Dennis – Rhythm Guitarist/Road Guitar Tech for B.B. King

Stacy Mitchhart – Singer/Guitarist Bluesman

Robert Garland – Amplifier/Guitar Tech – Founder Hillbilly Amplifiers

Huck Daniels – Guitarist previously with B.B. King

LaVerne Toney – V.P. – B.B. King Road Show Productions

Pat Foley – Gibson Artist Relations

Zachary R. Fjestad – *Blue Book of Electric/Acoustic Guitars*

Eric Ewin – Guitar Collector

Hartley Peavey – Founder/CEO Peavey Electronics Corp

Patty King – Daughter of B.B. King

Vincent (Red) Doss

INDEX